P9-DUM-698

INTRODUCING
AFRICAN WOMEN'S THEOLOGY

INTRODUCING

AFRICAN WOMEN'S THEOLOGY

Mercy Amba Oduyoye

INTRODUCTIONS IN FEMINIST THEOLOGY

EDITORIAL COMMITTEE

Mary Grey • Lisa Isherwood

Catherine Norris • Janet Wootton

The Pilgrim Press

Cleveland, Ohio

The Pilgrim Press, Cleveland, Ohio 44115

Co-published with Sheffield Academic Press Ltd, Sheffield, England

© 2001 Sheffield Academic Press

All rights reserved. Published 2001

Printed in Great Britain on acid-free paper

06 05 04 03 02 01   5 4 3 2 1

ISBN 0-8298-1423-X

Table of Contents

Editors' Preface

Introducing Feminist Theology is a BISFT (Britain and Ireland School of Feminist Theology) series committed to the global family of feminist theologies, as part of the universal struggle of women for justice and the recognition of full humanity. It is the hope that this book, *Introducing African Women's Theology*, the sixth in the series, will play a significant part in this process. It was a great joy when Professor Mercy Amba Oduyoye accepted the invitation to write it. Well-known in the Ecumenical Movement globally as well as for the way she opened up the Women's Desk in the World Council in Geneva and launched the Decade of Churches in Solidarity with Women, she has for many of us been the voice who brought the anguish of Africa to the Christian theological scene and refused to allow us to ignore the steadily worsening situation as Africa sank increasingly into poverty, debt, and the tragedy of AIDS.

This book is not only the vision of one woman theologian, inspiring though that may be. Although it does not claim to represent all the theologizing of African women from the 54 countries of the Organization of African Unity (OAU), it is very much an attempt to give voice to the growing community of African women theologians. Specifically, the book arises from the author's experiences between 1976 and 1996 when she made a sustained effort to discover and cultivate African women doing theology. This involved the creation of The Circle of Concerned African Women—and it is the lectures and papers from the Circle meetings which form a unique and precious resource for this book.

Professor Oduyoye poignantly depicts the context of African women doing theology: colonization and slavery form not only the background but the continuing struggle in the shape of racism, the increasing poverty engendered by globalization and neo-colonial economic structures. She shows how African women bring unique gifts to theology: the powerful tradition of story-telling means that theirs is narrative theology, drawing on oral traditions, myth, folk tale and of course the creativity of African women novelists.

Introducing African Women's Theology is not ivory tower theology, nor is it a book only for women. What Mercy Oduyoye conveys is African women's commitment to sustain life itself, a struggle born of the daily efforts of caring and nurture for the whole community. The significant contribution that it makes is the challenge to theology, liberation and the transformation of oppressive structures. In order to do this the book engages in a double hermeneutic: biblical hermeneutics is in dialogue with cultural hermeneutics. The reader is left in no doubt that the one is not possible without the other: a deep love of the liberating message of the Bible enables African women to draw out the transforming message to eradicate the injustice of a culture that still refuses full dignity to women. This method stimulates reflection on Christology, anthropology and ecclesiology. We are inspired by a vision of hospitality that extends to the hospitality of the earth herself.

The generosity of the author, her love for her people and country, and her vision of theology make this book unique. My hope is that the voices she has enabled through her book will never again be silenced, and that the longed-for transformation will be realized in her lifetime.

Mary Grey
(on behalf of the editorial committee)

Chapter One

Presenting the Study

Statement of Purpose

The particular theologies of African women express aspects of global and African Christian theologies from the vantage point of women's experiences and locations. They are the theologies that reflect women's heritage of participation in Africa's colonial and missionary history. They reflect the antecedent religion and culture which continue as Africa's religio-culture. This component of the context of Christian theology in Africa is one that plays a key role in women's theologies. The mercantile and colonial encounters with Arabs, Europeans and peoples of European descent, continue in Africa in terms of economic disadvantage flowing out of a history of enslavement and economic exploitation. The roots of poverty, racism and militarism are nourished by this history. Encounters with the propagators of Christianity and Islam have had a deep and pervading influence on the evolution of spirituality, religion and culture in Africa and continue to do so.

Given the geographical extent of Africa, and the diversity of Africa's peoples and historical experiences, there is a need to define the limits of the use of 'African' and 'African women'. The meaning of Africa, for the purpose of this study, is limited to countries from which have come the women's theological writings utilized in this study. No attempt is made to cover all of the 54 or so nations that belong to the Organization of African Unity (OAU).[1] This is done because the purpose of this book is to review the written sources of African Women's Christian theology

---

1. The countries of origin of the African women theologians whose words and/ or ideas appear in this publication are: Angola, Republic of Benin, Botswana, Burundi, Democratic Republic of the Congo (Zaire), Cameroon, Egypt, Ethiopia, Ghana, Kenya, Lesotho, Malagasy Republic, Namibia, Nigeria, Rwanda, Republic of South Africa, Swaziland, Tanzania, Togo, Zambia, Zimbabwe.

emanating from a particular source, namely, The Circle of Concerned African Women Theologians (The Circle).[2] Other religious perspectives and oral expressions are present only when necessary for comparative, collaborative or contrasting purposes, as their stance impinges on the community of understanding.

The word 'women' is limited to those who count themselves African and who believe that women have a desire and a responsibility to do their own thinking and to speak their own words about God as about all other religious and cultural concerns. The theology covers the writings of women who do not accept that African men's theology should suffice for the entire faith community. What we attempt to study here is African Christian Theology in the women-centered key.[3] There are expressions of faith from women alumnae of a variety of theological institutions as well as from other disciplines. Several are ordained into the Eucharistic ministry while others are lay theologians. All are keen churchwomen, and many have intensive liberative praxis and advocacy roles for the concerns that stimulate their theology. All together these are women whose theologizing go beyond the written word to liberative and transformative action. *Women* in this study refers to African women unless otherwise qualified.

Methodology

The narrative is mostly in the third person although I generally include myself in what I accept as efforts at offering liberating perspectives. I am therefore writing as a participant observer in this ongoing creative process. The first observation is that African women accept story as a source of theology and so tell their own stories as well as study the experiences of other women including those outside their own continent, but especially those in Africa whose stories remain unwritten. In this regard, the creative writings of African women have furnished a rich source of women's views on life as lived in Africa, thus providing the theologians with other perspectives on the context in which they theologize as well

---

2   The Circle of Concerned African Women Theologians was inaugurated in 1989 to facilitate research, writing and publication by a pan-African multireligious and multiracial network of women with a concern of the impact of religion and culture on African women.

3.   Theology is necessarily God-centered. Women-centered is to be understood as what highlights women as actors, agents and thinkers.

as how women from other disciplines interpret contemporary Africa. This framework is necessary, given the fact that narrative theology prevails in both oral and written materials. The normative role of stories in Africa's oral corpus, and the role of story in biblical theology, give women the paradigm for their theological reflection. Story was a traditional source of theology, which seems to have been superseded by analytical and deductive forms. It has taken the feminist movement to bring back the personal into academic studies and thereby revive the importance of the story. The approach to theology, that has characterized women, is to tell a story and then to reflect upon it. Some chapters will appropriate this method.

In doing theology women adopt a perspectival approach rather than analysis and critique of existing works. They grant that there are unique insights that come from individuals from contexts other than one's own and that there is something to be appreciated from that which is different. Other people's thoughts and arguments become stimulants, and not points of argument aimed at establishing what is definitive. Rather, the approach is that of dialogue as women aim at affirmations, continued questioning of tradition in view of contemporary challenges, and as they struggle with making their own contribution to the creation of theologies that respond to the demands of spirituality. There is very little refutation and apologetic to be gleaned from African women's theology. What is present are statements of faith and the basis for such affirmations.

Biblical Hermeneutics and African Culture

African women's theology constructed at their own pace, from their own place, portrays their priorities and perspectives. There has been an emphasis on survival, as they have to live so that they may be present in this life to struggle to disclose God's hand in their lives and in the actualities of Africa. Together, with the emphasis on context, is the place of the Bible. Skills for the interpretation of the Bible and culture from their own location have become a major challenge for women theologians especially as the Bible has become part of the African context. The need to distinguish the good that is liberating has turned the attention of many to biblical as well as cultural hermeneutics. Therefore, in theologizing, African women resort to tradition but they do so with skills for critical examination.

Cultural hermeneutics enables women to view the Bible through African eyes and to distinguish and extract from it what is liberating.

Since the Bible depicts other peoples' cultures, and we know from African culture that not everything in culture is liberating, we come to the Bible with the same cautious approach we have to culture. Any interpretation of the Bible is unacceptable if it does harm to women, the vulnerable and the voiceless. There are two sides to treating culture as a principle for hermeneutics. Taking culture as a tool with which to understand and interpret one's reality, and specifically the Bible, allows one to take one's experience seriously and to connect it with other realities. Culture is a broad concept, which always needs fine tuning, but in the African women's language, the broad description used for it is 'What human beings have made from nature, and because of nature and community'. All that is not nature has been 'cultivated', worked upon, devised, dreamed up, and given shape and meaning by the human mind and hands. *Culturing*, therefore, is a continuous activity of the human community, and culture has become the locus of resistance.

The other aspect of the appropriation of culture is evident in devising a hermeneutic of liberation to identify the positive aspects of culture and to promote them. The dynamism of culture demands that all take the responsibility to contribute to its evolution. So cultural hermeneutics directs that we take nothing for granted, that we do not follow tradition and ritual and norms as unchangeable givens, and that cultural relativism does not become covert racism and ethnocentrism. Life is to be lived deliberately, intentionally and consciously and where this practice has been lost we have to create awareness of life experiences and their implications. Experiences are to be analyzed, not only for their historical, social and ethical implications, but also for their capacity to create what grows to become cultural norms. African women have identified culture as a favorite tool for domination. That double culture leads to double oppression is the experience of all colonized peoples. In Africa, however, what we have to contend with is multiple cultures and multiple oppressions. In appropriating or critiquing culture, coping devices are discouraged as they only play into the patriarchal scheme. What we seek are strategies for transforming attitudes, beliefs and practices. We always ask of culture, how do I understand this experience, how does it relate to my context, who is benefiting? Is it just?

In cultural hermeneutics, one faces the challenge of struggling with one's culture while fencing off those waiting to use our culture to under-rate us. Cultural hermeneutics seeks a critique from within, and not an imposition from without. The challenge of cultural hermeneutics is the methodology. How does one recuperate historical memory, re-reading myths that are empowering while critiquing domesticating ones. We face the challenge of how to uncover the messages of cultural codes, myths, symbolisms and rituals, while never losing sight of the fact that contexts get more and more specific, the closer one gets to particular experiences and particular individuals.

Taking steps towards cultural hermeneutics we have found a few footholds on the path. There are no absolute truths in human affairs and human culture.

- Culture is frequently a euphemism to protect actions that require analysis.
- We need to interpret our own culture, engage in inter-cultural dialogue, and work towards cultural transformation.
- Keen sensitivity to the plurality of cultures and the dynamism of particular cultures is essential.
- Domesticating cultural practices thrive on the power of myth to go unchallenged, therefore 'Stop acting on these practices, and reflect on them.'
- Identify and promote what sustains and enhances life.
- Develop a keen sensitivity to the inherent dangers of tying identity to culture.

Illustrative of African women's concern for cultural hermeneutics are the writings of Oduyoye and Kanyoro. Oduyoye seeks parameters for identifying cultural elements that are life-affirming for women in Africa, whether they are validated by traditional Christian teaching or not. Key to this search is women's full humanity and participation in religion and society. Elements deemed incompatible with the gospel of fullness of life are studied for the cracks that may lead to transformation and the intransigence that call for prophetic condemnation. She allies cultural hermeneutics to biblical hermeneutics and finds this a very fertile area for imaginative theological reflection. Most African women use the Bible in very traditional ways following those of the schools of theology at which they studied. Several, however, have developed very creative ways of retelling biblical events so that they reflect the actual experiences of African women (Landman 1996).

Euro-American feminist theologians have alerted us to the hermeneutics of suspicion and that of commitment. The cultural hermeneutics being proposed combines both, as it shows African women taking a critical stance on African culture as well as promoting its commitment to wholeness and enhancement of life in the community. Cultural hermeneutics is the African women's way of taking seriously the issues of continuity and change. The pain of the depth of exclusion and victimization is placed before the plumb-line of the Good News of Jesus Christ which begins with the invitation to change, which will put people on the same course as that of the values in God's Great Economy.

In the face of Africa's peripheral role in the world and the legitimate anxiety of her further marginalization presented by globalization, women are often under pressure to keep silent about sociocultural aspects of life. There are African women and men who see any changes in women's participation and questioning of their legal and familial status as a threat to stability. Cultural hermeneutics exposes this situation and outlines ways of facing it creatively and with justice and compassion. Women theologians are not alone in the utilization of cultural hermeneutics. Creative writings by African women highlight much of what needs re-imagining in African culture. Through their poems, novels and drama they have offered analyses and critiques of African cultural practices.[4]

That women hold on to a cultural heritage that is said to uphold their dignity in their traditional society, calls into question the source of the yearning for dignity in practices of 'questionable benefit and real risk to health'.[5] For some, this raises the question of choice in anthropology. For others, it brings sexuality to the fore as a key factor in cultural hermeneutics; the more so as marriage is always discussed in African culture

---

4.   Florence Dolphyne, Professor of Language Studies, University of Ghana, cites the view of a consultation of African women held in Dakar, which produced what has come to be known as the 'Dakar Declaration'. The citation reads in part: '...aspects of our culture which discriminate, restrict and devalue women's physical, psychological and political development must be eliminated'. The debate here is how to do all this while maintaining national and ethnic traditions. Some of the writings that have been useful in this regard are by the following authors: Ama Ata Aidoo; Mariama Ba; Awa Thiam; Flora Nwapa; Buchi Emecheta; Nawal El Saadawi. The African women sociologists like Felicia Ekejiuba are also excellent sources for African women's lives.

5   This is a reference to the sensitive issue of female genital mutilation. Vibila Vuadi (Democratic Republic of Congo) and Nyambura Njoroge (Kenya) have attested to the practice of female genital operations, or surgery, which by their stance should be termed 'female genital mutilation'. This latter, abbreviated as FGM, would be the general stance of the women of The Circle, as they include the practice in their lists of 'Violence against Women'.

and in Christianity as if it concerns women only. It is with regard to marriage that women are discussed as if womanhood was a monochrome.

'Woman', 'Earth' and 'Africa' are all referred to in feminine terms. This is significant for our interpretation of women's experiences and therefore to the theological reflections they come up with. What Idowu says about Africa in relation to how 'she' fares on the global scene, is what I hear said about women:

> Where she behaves herself according to prescription and accepts an inferior position, benevolence, which becomes her 'poverty', is assured, and for this she shows herself deeply and humbly grateful. If for any reason she takes it into her head to be self-assertive and claim a footing of equality, then she brings upon herself a frown; she is called names; she is persecuted openly or by indirect means; she is helped to be divided against herself...a victim who somehow is developing unexpected power and resilience which might be a threat to the erstwhile strong (Idowu 1975: 77).

The uncanny resemblance between Africa as a continent of nations and the women who are Africans is what makes cultural hermeneutics an important aspect of the women's theology.

Paradigm Shifts

Though their theological heritage is made up of European and American theologies of various types, including missionary and feminist/womanist theologies, African women theologians take a critical distance from them, as their priority is to communicate African women's own understanding. Many participate in the Ecumenical Association of Third World Theologians (EATWOT) and, consequently, in the efforts of its women's commission. They are, accordingly, in collaboration with women theologians from Asia and Latin America. African women, therefore, acknowledge and share the concerns of several genres of women's theology but they do not necessarily work on identical themes, as the contexts are similar but not the same.

It is evident, for instance, that very few African women have struggled with the profound challenges of inclusive language although they relate positively to the issues being tackled. On the other hand, the traditional missionary perspective that Christianity is unqualified good news for Africa prevails in most of their writings, though some are critical of the outcome of Christianization and many take a critical stand towards the institutional expressions of the religion. It is to be observed, in addition, that Bible studies predominate, as connections between African culture and the world of the Hebrew Bible becomes clearer and clearer. Historical theology, with its sources in the Patristic, Medieval Dogmatics and the Reformation, has not played a significant role in women's theology. The stories utilized in the women's theology are from the Bible, Africa's history and culture, and from the women's own experiences of social change. They know that while history tells the 'high' stories, it is women who have to contend with the ground swell as well as the fall-out of the human story. The African women's theological reflections intertwine theology, ethics and spirituality. It therefore does not stop at theory but moves to commitment, advocacy and a transforming praxis.

The resources for the study of African women's theology are diverse. There are a number of individual reflections being published in journals of theology and church and ecumenical periodicals. One can also find most of the existing literature in anthologies governed by common themes, some of them being outcomes of communal research shared in conferences and consultations. A few individually authored books are also becoming available. Most frequent, however, is the oral mode, as women get the opportunity to share their reflections with study groups and conferences and in sermons. Those who have access to the unpublished 'Long essays' and projects in the Departments of Religion in African universities will also find a wealth of materials authored by women or on women. It is from these, but especially from the writings of women who belong to The Circle, that I derive the following description of African women's theology.

In their theological reflections, women of The Circle proceed from the narrating of the story to analyzing it to show how the various actors in the story see themselves, how they interact with others, and how they view their own agency in life as a whole. They ask 'What is the meaning of the story as a whole?' The next stage is to reflect on the experiences from the perspective of the Christian faith—a conscious implementation of biblical and cultural hermeneutics are at work in this process. From this perspective they identify what enhances, transforms or promotes in such a way as to build community and make for life-giving and life-enhancing relationships. The concern is not limited to the articulation of statements of faith. Women do theology to undergird and nourish a spirituality for life. And so from the affirmations of faith, which they make, issue in statements of commitment, flows the praxis that gives birth to liberating and life-enhancing visions and further actions and reflections.

This has led to the characterization of African women's theology as a theology of relations, replacing hierarchies with mutuality. It is therefore a theology that is 'society sensitive'. There is a marked emphasis on relations because African culture is very community-oriented and therefore requires all to be sensitive not only to the needs of others, but also to the well-being of the community as a whole.

Theology, therefore, has had to deal with the community in its manifestations of empowerment as well as its organized limitations on the individual and often on initiatives and innovations. Following from this is the characterization of inter-relationships. There is a theology of inter-relationship being developed as women emphasize the inter-relationship of women and men as well as that of humans and the rest of creation. This makes the theology ecologically sensitive, as all have to live, aware of the right of the other to a qualitative existence. As a theology developed in consciously multicultural and multireligious contexts, it is culture-sensitive and intentionally dialogue oriented. It undertakes dialogue between cultures as well as within cultures. With a developing cultural hermeneutic this theology boldly criticizes what is oppressive while advocating for the enhancement of what is liberative not only for women but for the whole community.

There is also a conscious effort to develop what is liberative in response to the social changes that challenge life in Africa. It is this project that involves African women in the praxis of the implementation of recommendations from research findings requiring a ministry of storytelling. Theology, whatever else it is, is also a story that is told, so that believers may become aware of God's presence in day-to-day life, and thereby make a choice whether or not they will walk with God. This is why the African women's theology has been described as 'a narrative theology' (Landman 1996). But their theology is also consciously perspectival, because its intention is to share the point of view of African women on issues that affect all of Africa, as well as those they consider as having global implications, even if they are generated outside Africa.

Traditionally, doing theology for the most part consists of knowing what others have written on your area of interest, doing your own listening and study of the contemporary scene and context, and finally having something to say on the issue. But the women's process does not end here, neither does it have to begin with reading other people's works, indeed most of the time the impulse to theologize is generated by experience or praxis. African women's theology does not end in documents, for the divorce of theology and ethics does not make for commitment and responsible living. This makes women seek a theology characterized by a struggle to make religion relevant to the challenges of contemporary Africa.

Since both the biblical sources and the African cultural sources lend themselves to multiple interpretations, African women have had to struggle with identifying and defining the principles of interpretation to be used in understanding their sources. Issues of particularity and universality are as critical to the understanding of Africa as they are to the understanding of all African sources. It is necessary to know what can be generalized for all Africa and what pertains to a single language or ethnic group. It is necessary to know the social location of the authors as well as the gender and other orientations from which they interpret experience. For women it has become clear that generalizing about Africa is most dangerous at the point where patriarchal ideologies are concerned. Certainly not all of Africa is patriarchal, but the hegemony of the patriarchal mind-set strives to make it so, and women have to resist this, as monolithic structures tend to be oppressive and the world cannot afford to do away with possible alternatives.

Women are developing cultural hermeneutics for the appropriation of Africa's religio-culture, which constitutes a resource for envisioning the will of God and the meaning of women's humanity. Theological messages, we suggest, are also coded into myths, folktales, proverbs, maxims and in ritual practices that are the common heritage of all Africans whatever their religious affiliation. The hermeneutics of culture takes into account culture as it has been touched by colonialism. Women, therefore, undertake a critique of the colonial culture's effect on women's lives and an appreciation and evaluation of the resilient elements of those of indigenous African origin. Here, African women share the liberation hermeneutics and feminist critique of dominant cultures. The challenge of cultural practices to how Christianity is lived in Africa, is one that women more than men have to wrestle with. Here, as in biblical studies, are hermeneutical questions that African women theologians have undertaken to explore and in response of which they seek tools of interpretation.

The second hermeneutical challenge, therefore, is the interpretation of Scripture. The question Philip put to the Ethiopian 'Do you understand what you read?' (Acts 8) is one that all theologians face. Women, fed on the understandings of men, are now doing their own reading. An area of great interest is, therefore, the study of the Bible. In this regard it is our experience as women that shapes our re-reading of the Scriptures. Women produce insights from their reading which are deep and speak more clearly to their situation. Naturally, there is an overlap of cultural and biblical hermeneutics as the Bible is most frequently read from the standpoint of African culture. Life-giving principles are extracted from both sources at the same time as their domesticating and death-dealing demands are repudiated as being against God's will for humanity and the rest of creation.

Sources

This book is based on experiences spanning the period from 1976 to 1996, two decades during which the author made an intentional bid to discover and cultivate African women doing theology. This initiative resulted in the creation of The Circle of Concerned African Women Theologians. The sources of the generalizations about African women's theology are in these two decades of meeting with individual women and groups of women. Initiating The Circle and establishing a team to promote its objectives meant intensive personal contacts and wide-ranging discussions to discover what are the key concerns of African women's theologies. The written sources for this work are mostly from anthologies of papers from conferences and consultations of The Circle, published, or in the process of being prepared for publication. In addition there is a good deal of material from oral sources, such as conversations on issues that many have reflected upon, a community tradition that cannot be properly attributed to one person. This will be the source of the generalized statements referred to above.

Where there is documentation, they have been cited in the normal way, but there is also material that derives from conferences and Bible study sessions, informal interviews and some personal letters that I have opted to keep anonymous. The main Circle sources are the Convocation of 25 September 1989 with the call 'Daughters of Africa Arise', and the Institute on 'African Women in Religion and Culture' which followed, from 26 September to 3 October. Secondly, I utilize the unpublished papers of the Pan-African Conference of The Circle which had the theme 'Transforming Power: Women in the Household of

God'.[6] Apart from these, over the two decades there have been publications and papers from national and zonal conferences of The Circle which are also available for this study. There are, of course, several unpublished theses, long essays and research papers which will provide the readers with further sources to enhance their understanding of African women's theology presented here in outline form and with selected themes only. These themes are:

- women's words about God—theology, narrowly defined
- Jesus, the divine-human—christological perspectives
- on being human—a Christian anthropology
- the household of God—studies in ecclesiology
- hospitality and spirituality—living the faith
- resurrection of the body—an eschatology.

There are of course several themes like suffering and sacrifice, ecology and missiology, which could have been chapters of this introductory work. The choice anticipates forthcoming publications as well as books already on the market.

My conclusions (Chapter 9, The Way Forward) embody my hopes and commitments. We are embarking on what we hope will be a liberative theology, going at our own pace, setting our own priorities and responding to our own contexts. Our immediate community of accountability is African women who seek a continent that is alive to God's mission in Africa and respond creatively to what God wills for Africans. Our visions are our own, but we do not close our eyes to similarities and commonalities across race, religion and nationality. At the same time we honor particularity and difference, and are sensitive to the patriarchal generalizations that fuel dualistic and oppressive ideologies. The 'we' in African women's theology is applicable where women struggle to disclose God's hand in their lives and in the African communities in which they participate.

The hermeneutics and fundamental principles of our interpretation of Scripture and culture are related to distinguishing the 'good'—that is, the liberation from the evil that is oppressive and domesticating and which puts limitations where none is necessary. We are re-reading our

6.   The papers delivered at the above conference will be published to provide further resources for the study of African women's theology described in this introductory work.

world, the texts that history has set before and around us. We acknowledge the variety of this tableau and the varieties of interpretations of our readings. We therefore have no presuppositions or illusions about a uniform African women's theology.

The stories we tell of our hurts and joys are sacred. Telling them makes us vulnerable, but without this sharing we cannot build community and solidarity. Our stories are precious paths on which we have walked with God, and struggled for a passage to our full humanity. They are events through which we have received the blessings of life from the hands of God. The stories we tell are sacred, for they are indications of how we struggled with God. While we were yet asleep or presumed dead, we heard the voice of Jesus saying *amka*! Those who declared us dead will see the resurrection of the image of God in the humanity of the African woman. We share our stories with you as people who believe that true community thrives where there is sharing in solidarity. While contributing to global solidarity we continue to nurture the traditional African women's solidarity that we have inherited from the countless generations of African women whose spirituality of resistance lives on in us.

Chapter Two

Significant Contexts of African Women's Theology

General Context

Theology is an expression of faith in response to experience. Biblical stories and events were narrated and transmitted not simply for entertainment nor for the purposes of historical records. They have been preserved as evidence that human life is in the hands of God and that God accompanies God's people through history, putting on them the obligation that they live to God's glory. Contemporary Christian theology in Africa—that is, the theology especially as it has evolved south of the Sahara—is a response to the Christianization of the past 300 years, in some places less. It has been, in the first place, a response to 'mission theology'. Secondly, it reflects the grappling with the social changes, which are inevitable as history moves ahead and human culture develops correspondingly, as well as in the shaping of this constant movement.

As written literature by Africans, it is less than half a century old and has been truly independent for less than half that time. Women have been agents in this experience of, and response to, the mission theology; a theology crafted to cope with the European endeavor to Christianize Africa in the context of slavery and colonization. As written theology, however, the women's theological contribution is even younger and takes its beginnings from the 1970s. It therefore has a span of life covering a mere two and a half decades. But this means that it is dynamic and vigorous, not easily trapped between the covers of a book. It also means that it cannot help but deal with life as lived in Africa, in the context of global challenges and situations that call for transformation. It is important to note from the outset that, for many, the African women's theology remains a story that is told, a song that is sung and a prayer that is uttered in response to experience and expectation. Women's theology is, therefore, evolving in the context of the challenge to make theology reflect what Christians in Africa understand God to be about. Women's theology is a significant contribution to African theology. It issues out of academies, theological institutions, pulpits, Church statements from Church leaders and councils, as well as from the lyrics sung in Church and cassettes sold in the streets of Africa, for it ensures the inclusion of women's experience in the faith statements of Christianity in Africa.

The primary context of women's theology, therefore, is that of an effort to make a contribution so that Christian theology in Africa will be a word of both women and men, lay and ordained, teachers and preachers, poets and sculptors.

Secondly, this theology has the whole of life for a context. Women's theology is crafted in the midst of the ongoing life in Africa, over-shadowed by economic exploitation, political instability and militarism. African women have to extract meaning from it all. They have to see and live life whole. They experience three major religious structures and varieties of cultures, traditional and imported. Life is lived as a whole: thus understanding birth as a gift from God, the Source Being; as the return of an ancestor; as an addition to the workforce; as a mouth to feed and a personality to develop and tend; and as a human being in the image of God to socialize into a global citizen. Theology has to reflect all this. Since the 1960s the drama of Africa has been the attempt to transform colonial economies into national ones that participate in the global structures not only to the advantage of 'the other', but also for the development and nourishing of Africa's people. The drama of poverty has altered much of Africa's traditional norms of human relationships, which consisted of upholding the dignity of the human and the integrity of creation. It emphasized the building of caring communities, nurturing reciprocity and mutuality, and respecting the rest of nature.

Today, the struggle for survival has overshadowed traditional under-standing of the quality of life, which taught that life is to be lived in respectful relation to God, the Spirit World, nature and other human beings. The African women's theology cannot but reflect this poverty syndrome by working to construct a liberating theology. In this regard we do need to remember that Africa harbors Christian theologies of many types, some liberative while others are domesticating, urging Afri-cans to conform to the demands of an exploitative global economic structure. While economies change, while the local becomes globalized, African culture evolves social structures to cope. Life and relationships

before the era of television, fast travel, mega churches and mega economies, is vastly different from the contexts in which the pre-modern
culture developed. Modernity in Africa means the demands of Islam,
missionary Christianity and globalization. All of this has meant transformation of meanings, especially with regard to the concept of community.

In the midst of these challenges African women carry on a mothering
agenda, seeking to nourish the economically disadvantaged and socially
marginalized people, as well as those blatantly discriminated against
because of color or ethnicity. They see themselves as the custodians of
life, sustainers of community, the transmitters and upholders of culture.
African women's theology bears the marks of the creation of a people
whose human rights are trampled over. They are women who are
doubly and triply burdened, women whose humanity needs to be proclaimed. This is an area where women of Africa have numerous stories
to share. Stories of poverty, exploitation, violence and racism are con-
stants in the contexts of theologizing. Analyzing these stories reveals
how religio-cultural ideas, that foment ethnocentrism, brew the evil and
sin with which theology struggles. Religious ideas of destiny and witchcraft leave some women unable to resist exploitation and dehumanization, accepting them as unchangeable givens ordained by God. The
context of religion and culture deserve further elaboration, as they constitute the main arena of women's research and writings.

Religio-cultural Context

There are classic elements in African culture that women take into
account in their theological reflection. By classic elements we refer to
aspects of culture that seem to be Africa-wide, as well as those of endur-
ing nature which have demonstrated resilience against 'invading' cultures
and against conscious efforts at cultural and religious colonization. This
cultural heritage does not have an impact on women and men in the
same way or to the same extent; hence the need to examine 'woman's
culture' within the general cultural experience of Africans. We also need
to keep in mind that this rich heritage is not uniform, and that the
impact of Asia, Europe and Arabia varies from place to place, as does
that of Christianity and Islam. Internal migration patterns, some following the demise of ancient empires and kingdoms, are factors to be recognized in any study of the evolution of African culture. This limited
study, however, only deals with elements that may be observed in
contemporary Africa.

We also need to note at the outset that we are dealing with a religion-based culture. Africans live in a spiritual universe. Whatever has an outward appearance also has an inner essence and we have to stay in touch with God from whom we came to inhabit this dimension of reality. The traditional way of life is closely bound up with religion and religious beliefs in such a way that there is a mutual interdependence of religion and culture. We note in the second place that African Religion provides a holistic view of life. It enables persons to understand and accept their status and identity and passes on beliefs that explain prevailing conditions. African Religion teaches its adherents how to survive and thrive in the world in which they have been placed. This religion undergirds the shaping of the moral, social and the political, and even, at times, the economic. Hence, the moral obligations that weigh so heavily on African women are firmly hooked on to beliefs.

African Religion does not claim to be a 'revealed religion'. It consists of intimations about nature, traditions handed down about the nature of the world, the origin and place of human beings in the scheme of things, the beliefs concerning the existence and role of the ancestors and the spirits of nature, which all converge into a religio-culture that rules and directs life in Africa, and makes lineage and kinship powerful controlling factors in the lives of Africans. I use the present tense because this control continues to affect all with different intensities, but especially women whose image and social status continue to be anchored largely in the perpetuation of lineages through marriage and child bearing. For both women and men it is marriage that promotes the person into the status of a responsible adult. For women theologians, therefore, marriage becomes an inescapable context for theology and is itself a theological issue. It is important to note that the family and the whole community constitute the context in which this religio-culture is imbibed. In both contexts, the voice of the ancestor is said to hold the key to personal and community well-being. Therefore, the African women theologians, seeking to identify the ultimate authority that governs their lives, ask, 'whose voice is the voice of the ancestor?'

African Religion belongs to the people—they are born into it, and to date not much has emerged that may be identified as a missionary impulse. On the other hand, some Africans have chosen to adopt other religions, mainly Christianity and Islam. Nevertheless, the cultural norms remain traditional—that is, for significant aspects of life, people follow what has been handed down by former generations, changing whatever is necessary in order to suit the changing circumstances. My concern here is to examine this change in relation to African women's lives. Women have been taught to comply with the demands of religion with the understanding that thereby they re-align themselves to the source of their being.

Although there are no 'scriptures' that claim that the tenets of African Religion were revealed by God, the tradition of religious demands persists as that to which our forebears adhered in order to survive and prosper, and as that which they expect us to abide by. Whether religion is of human origin or not, the belief is that it is what holds a community together in harmony and well-being and therefore constitutes what God wills for humanity. Religious order is therefore treated as given by God. Laws of nature, moral precepts, are believed to originate from God and are monitored by the 'departed' or 'living-dead' for the well-being of all living beings. Human beings are held responsible for the well-being of all creation as human action is believed to affect the rest of nature. For example, nature responds with abundance and generosity or with devastation and withdrawal of beneficence to the acts of omission or commission that emanate from humans. Hence there are several taboos concerning days of rest and ritual cleaning up of one's environment. The belief that humans come from God and return to God governs many personal and communal rites especially those related to birth and death.

Another cardinal cultural trait is the 'communal' ideology. A human being is born into a human community, and that is what makes him or her human. African anthropology sees humans as beings who depend on life-in-community for their self-understanding. This has been passed down in the maxim 'I am, because we are' which means that, for the African, 'the personal is communal'. This is the context in which one finds women adhering to traditional norms while men move into individualistic ways of life, seemingly with impunity. Women seek to understand men's shift and women's continuing adherence. In pre-colonial Africa, the worst punishment to be meted out to anyone was exile. It was deemed worse than judicial execution. It is also for this reason and in this context that all separation events are ritualized and celebrated. And yet individualism seems to be gaining ground among Africans, especially among men. Women theologians ask 'Why?'.

Further, there is the celebration of life, which characterizes life among Africans. The spirituality of Africans is rooted in fullness of life. Life and more life is the prayer of African Religion, hence the belief that we attain immortality through our descendants. Every aspect of life is celebrated. All beginnings and endings are marked by ritual. All signs of abundance and renewed health are celebrated. Life is to be lived with full intent, lived forcefully and with power. Celebration of life is seen in festivals, which often call on women to provide feasts. The ultimate concern of all this is for fullness and blessedness of life. Those who are blessed demonstrate their appreciation of their good fortune by being hospitable to others. This makes hospitality a religio-cultural trait of Africans. Giving, to ensure life and to preserve the life-force or save the 'face' of others, is part of African culture. Sharing is built into communal existence, but it does not remain there. All strangers, living or passing through, become the responsibility of the host community. This principle of hospitality is based on honoring reciprocity. In contemporary Africa, this is an aspect of culture most challenged by Westernization, poverty and the lack of reciprocity.

That colonization of Africa was an invasion of African culture is self-evident. In many places it succeeded in demolishing traditional political structures. Almost everywhere it undermined the social relations and, together with Christianization, assumed that cultural practices could be judged at the courts of European culture and be dismantled, validated or enhanced according to European norms. Most fundamental of this cultural re-orientation is the Western philosophy of individualism. In religious terms this is translated as individual salvation but it did not change social and cultural obligations which are communal in nature. Certainly not for women.

The Power of Culture

Christianity offers a way of life. It is therefore a global culture, albeit one that varies a great deal because it evolves in relation to existing ways of life. It opposes, it adapts, it adopts and it transforms, while it is itself opposed, adopted, adapted, challenged and transformed by the host cultures. The culture of the Swiss Calvinist is not the same as the German Lutheran, and both are distinct from the Roman Catholic, although all three belong to the ancient Christianity of the Western Roman empire, and are all culturally distinct from the Christian cultures of Kerala in South India, Armenia, Greece, Russia, Egypt and Ethiopia. The Christian culture with which we are dealing in this book takes its impulses from Western European Protestant and Roman Catholic norms. There is, therefore, a wide variety of the material culture of these forms of Christianity in Africa. The liturgies, tunes, poetry, prayers, robes and pipe organs, wedding cakes and burial caskets, all of these may be points for discussion as to the part they play in women's lives and women's evaluations of them. Inculturation in missiology is a component of African women's theology, especially as Western cultures bring with them a markedly patriarchal ideology.

In Africa's history, the arrival of Western Christianity was an assault on the African way of life launched by ethnocentric Europeans in collaboration with colonial administration and colonial violence. This colonization has not ended. In fact new forms of Christianity are arriving in Africa with even more trenchant antipathy for Africa's indigenous religio-culture. The arrogant Christianity that arrived in Africa from Europe saw, in the spirituality of African cultures, nothing but idolatry. This situation continues in certain forms of Christianity that are currently sweeping Africa.

The intolerance of difference within cultures and within religious communities, is one that women theologians have often commented upon. Their critique of culture applies as much to the Western Christian culture as to the African religio-culture, not excluding the Islamic. Both are two-edged swords. Culture is experienced by women as a tool for domination, but there are aspects that can be liberative so they do not undertake a wholesale condemnation of either. They have to contend, however, with the fact that the Western Christian culture and patriarchal ideology have seeped in, to enhance the power of men or to endow men with power where they had none, while suppressing aspects of African culture that are favorable to women.

Women often cite Western education as a positive aspect of this encounter as it has been the vehicle for introducing a wider spectrum of choice in the economic field. They note the Church's role in attempting to Christianize African culture, but not without pointing out that in many instances the Church's prohibitions are often ineffectual, and that in actual fact Christianity promises more than it delivers. Yet there is ample evidence that what diminishes woman is perpetuated and enhanced even by Christianity and by some women. At the same time, a culture of silence over repressive elements is the norm for women. Contemporary social change in Africa is characterized by a further assault on African culture by evangelical missions and the global technological culture, both of which have no respect for these traditional taboos. It is not our aim to speculate but rather to take these developments in hand and to transform them so that they can be the tools for justice and compassion.

African women recognize cultural plurality and the necessity to honor and celebrate difference as long as practices do not entail injustice and violence. But they would like to see this not only across cultures but also within them. Further, they realize that to live creatively they must dispense with ethnic superiority, relativize the Christian culture and admit that paradigm shifts are inevitable and that reconstruction is the duty and prerogative of each generation. They hold that an unshakable principle in cultural critique is the dignity of human beings and the sacredness of life. Women's theology shows a keen awareness of the fact that 'the past' is often misused for the subjugation of women, while traditional values that are advantageous to women and ecology are overlooked. Hence, to do theology women have to seek new norms with all assiduity. They struggle to unmask the patriarchal powers in order that women might be empowered to share their perspectives as well as reconstruct their self-esteem.

Women's theology is crafted in the contexts of women's solidarity. In the community of women none is treated as an object. Women all recognize mutual dependence, support and correction. They see themselves as having embarked on a joint search for relevance. Convinced that one head does not constitute a council, they consult together so that their chances of arriving at reliable sources and construction may be heightened. They act together hoping that in so doing they might improve their chances of coming closer to the realities of their lives and hopefully closer to the truth that will set them free, creating a community in which the image of God in women will be honored.

Socialization

A prevalent concern in the context of theology is the method of transmitting value. Between what is 'natural' and what is socially acceptable, we try to balance what makes us who we are. Human communities have become very complex, and impulses making us who we are come to us not only from family, neighbors and schools, but also from television and commerce, which open the way for the whole globe to have the possibility of influencing us. The nations and the communities we live in are themselves variegated. So the possibility is open for us to build our self-image on persons other than those of our families or primary culture. In spite of this backdrop, one can still defend the validity of traditional understanding of socializing agents as being parents, peer group, school and the general public. What women theologians examine especially are the factors that go into making an African woman.

Pluralism and multiculturalism are as evident in African cities and small towns, as they are elsewhere, but beneath this veneer is the socialization that is achieved through cultural education. Socialization comes through the observance of rewards and sanctions, through admonitions and warnings backed by stories and examples. The inculcation of how to live in harmony with your community and your environment and to avoid shame on one's self and one's kin, is the aim of socialization. Both boys and girls are socialized into their specialized gender roles. Concepts of femininity and masculinity, by which they will be guided in adult life, are heavily culture coded and therefore need to be taught. Socialization is aimed at seeking a balance between the life and well-being of the individual and that of the community. It is to promote what the community accounts good and honorable and a source of blessing for the past, present and for posterity.

The process of socialization is very often one of informal learning by sheer fact of participation in the community. However, direct guidance is given by adults and peer groups, which bring the young to conform to societal norms or bear the consequences. In this process all are witnesses to what happens to deviants, as well as the fact that occasionally people 'get away with' non-conformity and even blaze new trails. In general, however, the adult wish is that their offspring stand out only if it is for achieving greatness, not notoriety. Proverbs, maxims and other wise sayings with which Africans lace their daily speech are carriers of these cultural expectations. They are the pegs on which the community hangs its mores. They are treated as truisms to make people adhere to the style of life that custom has come to expect of them because of gender or other status-specific differentiations.

There are, on the other hand, identifiable instances and events which demand that cultural practices are taught. These are most often associated with the life-cycle. Here we note that women theologians have called attention to the rituals of these observances that affect women's lives and which make them aware of what it means to be a woman in an African community. A well-studied instrument of socialization in Africa is the preparation for marriage. Most communities have intentional educational events which take place throughout childhood but specifically at the threshold of adulthood, in what has become generally known as initiation rites. The result of this socialization, and especially as related to the latter, is that African women are programmed to live for others. They live for children, family and community as these constitute the locus of one's worthiness. This in some cases has come to mean that women live to please men and pride themselves with being the providers of continuity and the carriers of tradition. For the women, therefore, critique of norms of womanhood are part of the theology (Ravelonolosoa Diambaye 1996). These preoccupations are also present in the creative literature (Ogunyemi 1996: 15).

Meanwhile, we examine hospitality and communion, we dream of working for the elimination of injustice and violence and we continue to struggle with how the images of womanhood rule our lives. Layers of legal provisions in Africa—traditional, colonial and post-colonial—all have a way of being adhered to by different people and are more often than not to the detriment of women's self-esteem. There are beautiful images that put women at the core of family, such as the proverbs which proclaim that unmarried adult men are not complete because they are men without women. On the other hand, there are many other sayings, such as 'there is no woman as beautiful as the obedient one' and 'women are the servants of men', which women cannot help but object to if they have any sense of self. But these are nothing compared with the verbal violence against women that is found in song, proverb and other folktalk. The popular use of biblical texts and the mass media ignore the humanity of women and focus on their biological make-up. Where women decide to rid themselves of these pictures, they talk in terms of walking together with Jesus. And soon they have to deal with the fact that this Jesus, whom they wish to accompany, has his face set towards Jerusalem, for confrontation and trial: hence the concern for a theology of sacrifice as well as the meaning of being created in the image of God.

Theological Concerns

Foregoing context has yielded several concerns that have become the issues for women's theology as they are for the study of other aspects of life in Africa and the content of the literature composed by African women creative writers. Given the emphasis on relationships in Africa, culture has become a key issue in women's theology, and with that the concern for community, hospitality and multireligious living. Examining the relationship between women and men has led to a focus on religious anthropology. Explanations of humanness offered by African Religion, as well as that of Christianity, are being examined by women. This has become necessary because both the communal ideology and the rites of passage that highlight it impinge most significantly on the lives of women. It is from this experience of the traditional anthropologies that women have found it necessary to also re-examine the speculations on the origins of the world.[1]

Myths of creation, mostly theological, spell out the unity and whole-ness of nature and human nature. They include the thread of life that binds God, spirit beings and human beings in a relational triangle, the constant communication that is generated and required by this commu-nity of life, the grace and the compassion of the Source Being, the dig-nity of the human being and the sacredness of the principle of life and all of life. All of these have become the major theological concern of African women.

Negation of community and attacks on life are seen as evil. Whatever threatens human survival is feared: it is evil and is to be abhorred and exorcised. These attacks are sinful because they undermine the worthi-ness of the Source Being, the sacredness of life and the dignity of the human being. Evil manifests itself in witchcraft, the aberrations of life and attacks on what makes for well-being. Women have focused atten-tion on Jesus of Nazareth as restorer of harmony and the model of the human as God intended. Women's Christology centers around goodness, salvation, liberation and the acts that redeem, transform or reconstruct. Their religion is a quest for freedom and blessedness: the complete and integral well-being that the Yoruba of Nigeria describe as *alafia* and the Hebrew render as *shalom* and for which the Muslim women theologians have taught their Christian sisters to render in Arabic as *salaam*.

Christian women theologians in Africa have also turned their atten-tion to the Church with a concern for its redemption from the patriar-chal captivity that undermines its Christlikeness. Justice and participation are key words in *koinonia*, the women's paradigm for ecclesiology. Their experiences of life have led to an examination of how they struggle for survival and the sources of the impulses that make them seek to enhance

---

1.   For a helpful summary of these, see Mazrui 1986: 296-301.

life for others. This has led to reflections on spirituality, suffering and sacrifice. Theology for African women is about living rightly and putting things right, hence the element of hope in their constructions. In addition, theology is for them a statement of faith enabling them to live their tomorrow today, as they await new life, the resurrection of the life of God in the midst of all creation beginning with us, humans made in God's image.

Surveying the contexts we come to some understanding of the choices of theological themes by African women. They are confronted daily with issues of community and wholeness. They do their reflections in the context of multireligious and multicultural living. Their culture demands that they stay sensitive to relatedness and inter-relatedness. It follows from this that they reflect on the reciprocity, mutuality and justice that community life demands. Woven into all this is hope, the reason for struggling. These givens of the African contexts have provided the agenda for the theology of African women and of women's religious discourse. I conclude the survey with a few notes on women's experience of struggling in hope.

Community and Wholeness

The general low level of material development in most African countries and the continued economic disadvantages, in terms of global transactions, has resulted in the tendency to perpetuate the image of Africans as living in poverty. On the other hand, Africans live a wish to perpetuate the traditional norms of a caring and sharing community. This has put the burden of community and individual wholeness on a few who are seen to have 'made it' economically and who are also 'traditional' enough to feel that they have obligations towards others. Where women are concerned, this obligation becomes an inescapable demand if they are to be at peace and fully integrated into their communities.

Harmony and integrity are principles that are highly prized in African culture. Living in harmony with nature, for example, derives from religious speculations that link the human, the natural and the divine, and which makes God the source of all life. Life is an integrated whole and human beings ought to live recognizing and reflecting this integrity in their own lives and in their lives-in-community. The respect for life, the connectedness and the need to stay in communication, has meant that by and large multireligious and multicultural living are taken for granted.

Africans recognize that every community is a community of communities and not a melting pot. Whatever is adopted, adapted, assimilated or ignored comes from a gradual interaction and not from imposition. But for the hegemonic ideas from Christianity and Islam there will be very little conflict in Africa that has religious origins. People convert to ideas and styles of life because they make sense. That is, they generate more life or enhance the good that already exists. Community does not remain static, but that it should be a source of wholeness and of *alafia*, is for Africans an unalienable principle.

The sense of community characterizes traditional life in Africa and in spite of modernization, moves people to care for children, the aged, strangers, the sick and the needy, widows, disabled and others deemed vulnerable. The religio-culture is a common base for ethical and moral choices that highlight obligations and responsibilities. The *alafia* of the individual is bound up with that of the community. Women comply with the demands of community in the hope that their own *alafia* will be seen to. Seeing to the needs of community in Africa includes participation in religious observances and practices, which constitute the base for ethical and moral choices.

Wholeness is used here to mean all that makes for fullness of life, and makes people celebrate life. Well-being—*alafia*—for most of Africa implies the possession of the powers, graces or attributes that call for the celebration of life, and demonstrates the integrity of the human body, good eye-sight, hearing and speech and the wholeness of mind and limbs. Africans consider human beings as enjoying fullness of life when they have good health and the power to procreate. This latter is seen as a religious duty. Fullness of life is defined as a state of prosperity, victory over evil and death-dealing forces. Rains and harvest, harmony with nature, all call for thanksgiving and celebration. When such a state prevails, life is whole and the whole creation enjoys *alafia*.

The search for wholeness leads Africans to respect multicultural and inter-religious approaches to life in community. There is admiration for how others achieve that wholeness and especially for the religions that undergird the perspectives on wholeness and the means to attain that state.

Relatedness and Inter-relationships

Ecological, social and economic realities derive from the belief in and the experience of unity of the community. The fact that has generated ecological sensitivity in Africa is human dependence on nature for food, energy and shelter. The religion that emerged in Africa was developed to ensure harmony between the elemental forces and humans. Rivers are kept clean, lagoons are dredged, trees are preserved and harvests are celebrated in gratefulness for the provisions of nature. The sea, the rains and the hills are all recognized as contributing to the well-being of humans. Various members of the world of plants and animals, and aspects of earth's physical features have special relations to specific groups of people, because of mythic, legendary and historical experiences. Many plants are held in high esteem for providing healing substances. Humanity's well-being depends on the harmonious relationship of the whole creation, and human culture evolves from the utilization and adaptation to the natural environment.

Arising out of this ecological relationship is the spiritual connectedness. The belief that creation has a divine origin is accompanied by a belief in the sacredness of nature and of the physical world as providing locations for spirit-beings. Hence plants and animals, hills and mountains, and rivers and lakes become associated with divine beings, together with the spirits of the departed human beings, the ancestors, which constitute one side of the 'triangle of reality'. In the African religious worldview, God, the Source Being, other-spirit beings, as described above, and human beings are in constant communication and inter-relationship. This relatedness and inter-relationship controls and directs human actions and relationships. On the horizontal level, kinship and lineage descent, and political alliances between 'jural communities', define relationships and relatedness.

The variety of approaches to the sacred in African Religion leads Africans to respect the religions of others and indeed to adopt aspects that enhance their own religious beliefs and practices. Religion is a means to the end of fullness, and women's struggles include following religious practices in order to preserve life or to ensure its continuation. All viable alternatives to securing *alafia* are deemed legitimate. Options are respected unless there is a factor of exclusivism, such as was introduced by Christianity and Islam. Even then, there have developed African adaptations of these religions that include aspects of Africa's religio-culture.

Although there are unifying threads in African culture, the most obvious fact is its variety, as evidenced in the thousand different languages of the continent. Africans, therefore, have a tendency to assume multiculturalism. In the modern state, as carved by colonial presence, several cultural varieties co-exist with no attempt at uniformity being imposed. Tanzania is a significant exception. A case in which the adoption of one language, Swahili, and the reorganization of traditional land utilization and settlement following political independence, has resulted in the observation that younger Tanzanians rarely speak the language of their grandmothers. When ethnic languages fall into disuse the likelihood is that many local cultural practices may atrophy and disappear. Mostly, Africans who are rooted in their ethnic cultures respect others for doing the same. In cultural change, more than in religion, there is more dynamism in the interaction and in personal rites. The general tendency however has been to conserve the variety of cultures. This makes for a lively context in which to do theology.

Reciprocity and Justice

The political systems that undergird traditional African community were diverse; therefore, none could survive without reciprocal obligations, and without oiling the wheels of relationships with the recognition of the worth and the needs of the other. This ensured that Africans worked with the principle that relatedness and inter-relatedness call for reciprocity and justice. Unlike the colonial politics, which were virtual dictatorships, traditional government was based on representation and consultation, with a provision for the elimination of rulers and elders who exhibit dictatorial tendencies or lack of compassion for the ruled. Both rulers and the ruled are bound by covenants. Throughout African communities the moral obligations enforced include reciprocity and justice. In contemporary Africa, the superimposition of outside influences has brought much confusion. The individualism that has been pitched against communalism, and dualistic philosophies, has become an ally for Africans who want to shirk communal well-being, justice and reciprocity. Women theologians therefore ask 'what does a woman brought up with a sense of community do in the face of this encroaching egoism?' Is there 'a word from God' for such a context?

The injustice that women experience has become the context of their theology. Women find societies unjust because, for the greater part of their existence, women are taken for granted. They are marginalized or given secondary roles not commensurate with their skills or qualifications. Women experience the injustice of being blamed for whatever does not go right. The injustice of having to implement decisions they did not help to make, the injustice of having to struggle to have one's humanity recognized and treated as such, all of this becomes the context of struggle reflected in women's theology.

Compassion and Solidarity

Hurting with those who hurt, and rejoicing with those who are enjoying life, is an important aspect of women's theology. In women's lives it is this compassion that is at work in the self-giving care that is expected of them and which most give without counting the cost. Compassion is the well spring of women's solidarity that is evident in the many women's organized groups, both in traditional society and the contemporary women's movements. For women theologians the existence of strong women's groups within the Church gives them both a community of accountability and a locus of resource for theologizing. This sensitivity to the actual prayers of African women has meant that women theologians have a strong focus on marriage, family life and especially on the child factor. This seems to be a distinctive mark of African women's concerns and therefore a crucial theological issue.

Since procreation is an experience that has great influence in their lives, birth and birth-giving feature prominently in the religious ritual with which they have to deal and also, therefore, in their theological reflections. It is the hope of bringing into being the next generation that maintains the institution of marriage. The precarious situation of medical attention during pregnancy and birthing and the continued high level of infant mortality have meant that hope is the main resource for a woman's struggle. The hope for new life is not only figurative in Africa, it is actual, it is also a hope for transformation that keeps women struggling. Circumstances will change for the better. If they continue to struggle, their daughters and sons may grow up to live in a better world. Hope is the reason for the struggle. But in what is such a hope anchored? That is the subject of the next chapter.

Through most of women's struggling and theologizing, it is only by the grace of God that women survive the ordeals of life to continue to be true life-givers. It is by the grace of God that they are able to hope and have reason to struggle on the side of *alafia*, specifically as women with a mothering agenda. Mothering is a term to encapsulate not simply biological motherhood, but all the nurturing, mentoring and life-enhancing praxis that make for humanity and human communities as women imagine God to have willed and of which the Gospel provides a glimpse. Mothering is an obligation for all in any community whether they are women or men. It is doing to others what God does to, with, and for us out of God's compassion. In women's lives it is this compassion that is at work in the self-giving care that is expected of them and which most give without counting the cost.

Summary

In Africa, Christian theology of the past four decades has reflected the experience of and response to 'mission' theology. It has also reflected the social changes occurring, which are inevitable as history moves ahead and human culture develops, responding to as well as shaping this constant movement. African women's theology is developing in the context of global challenges and situations in Africa's religio-culture that call for transformation.

Chapter Three

Women's Word about God

From our Stories

Growing up
in my father's house
at the missionary's feet
I saw you as a
grey-bearded white man from far
a large all-seeing
all-knowing
EYE

Stern and demanding
throw away your brass and stone idols, they said
He is a jealous God
serve no one but He
Burn your totems and
change your name
save your soul from
Heresy (Govinden 1997: 148).

Re-imaging God is an exercise that all African Christians have been forced to go through. This poem by Betty Govinden tells the story which you will find in all missiological studies relating to Africa. It is no different for women. However, for women there are additional dimensions that need investigating. This is what this chapter will attempt to introduce. In the eyes of Christian missionaries, African Religion was nothing but idolatry. Reflecting as it does in all of the culture, phenomena such as naming had to be abandoned to ensure that names of idols are not carried into the house of the 'jealous God' of Christianity. It is for this reason and the fact that the African Religion continues that we begin our 'God-talk' by rehearsing what we learn from African Religion.

In the worldview of Africans, creation originates from the divine realm and life is therefore held as sacred. Since theology is about God, the divine realm, the sacred and our human presence in the scheme of things, we open our theological discourse with creation stories which in Africa appear mainly as God's story. In creation stories we find concepts such as the wholeness, unity, relatedness and inter-relatedness of all that exists. We also discover the belief that since God is the source of life and being, all life is to be held as sacred and therefore worthy of respect. The worth-ship of the maker reflects on what has been made, and nothing is to be deemed trivial and unworthy of existence and therefore to be excluded from the enjoyment of fullness of life. From these beliefs flow some of the cardinal themes of African women's theology. From creation stories, we discern and interpret the presence of the divine and unique Source Being, known in Africa by many names. In the Hebrew Bible, the name is Yahweh, to Christians using English and related languages, the name is God and to the Moslem and the Arabic-speaking world, the name is Allah.

When humans experience the absence of life, they discern and interpret the situation as the absence of God. People seek explanation of the absence through myths of separation of heaven and earth or the withdrawal of God to the upper realms of the cosmos. This absence spells death to all that exists and death is viewed as contrary to the will of the 'one who created life' and so is attributed to a primordial communication between God and humanity that went askew. At the same time numerous maxims affirm the continued presence of God with creation and particularly with human beings. In theology Africans speak of God as source, reason and end of existence. They see God as the source of *alafia* (Yoruba word meaning *shalom*), grace, hospitality and compassion. For women, therefore, the 'sacred' becomes a source of strength to encounter and overcome the obstacles to life, which sprouts before them in the context in which they do theology. The Fulani—an ethnic group akin to the Berbers of North Africa, and found throughout the savannah belt of West Africa—are nomadic cattle herders who have become Islamized. The Fulani believe that the world was created from a drop of milk:

> At the beginning there was a huge drop of milk.
> The Doondari came and he created the stone
> Then the stone created iron;
> Then iron created fire;

> Then fire created water;
> Then water created air.
> The Doondari descended the second time,
> Took the five elements
> And shaped them into the human one (Beier 1966: 1).

There are many such myths, depicting the beginning of 'all things'. Several of these include the creation of male and female humans or the origins of the differentiation of the sexes. The Fang of Gabon say: 'At the beginning of things, when there was nothing...Nzame made everything... When Nzame finished everything that we see today, Nzame called Mebere and Nkwa (the male and the female) and showed them the work' (Beier 1966: 18).[1]

In African myths human beings are usually created after other aspects of nature that have been brought into being. The following dramatic description comes from Nigeria:

> In the beginning Woyengi seated herself on a stool
> And with her feet firmly planted on the creation stool
>   and a table before her,
> She began to mould human beings out of earth (Oduyoye 1995: 23).

Sometimes the Originator of humanity is a man, as in the Yoruba Obatala, at other times a woman, as in the Chewa Namalenga, but nothing happens by chance. All are created by the deliberate will, action or word of the Supreme Being, known by many names. Creation stories are told as God's stories, since in them we discern what God transmits to us when we look around us and wonder 'the how' and 'the why' of our presence in creation and of creation in its totality. When we theologize, we are trying to articulate our belief in the divine origin of all that is and its concomitant of the sacredness of all being. The *Enuma Elish*, versions of which are found in the Qur'an and in the Hebrew Bible, are pivotal for African women, Christian and Muslim alike, as they attempt to God-talk as well as God-walk. But they are challenging its role as the definitive story in their lives given that they live in contexts that provide them with other stories. Nonetheless, from this foundation story of the

---

1.   Nzame, Mebere, Nkwa are a divine triad now merged together under Nzame. Another traid is found in Uganda among the Ankole. Here they are in fact triplets (brothers)—Nyamuhanga, Kazooba Nyamuhanga and Rugaba Rwa Nyamuhanga. A Tanzanian story which makes 'The Word' the force that enabled one thing to create another, and is an unseen entity, is noteworthy for the purposes of the reconstruction of mythology (Beier 1966: 42-46).

Semitic world flows the central attitudes to life that inform their theology: sacredness of life, the relatedness and inter-relatedness of all, mutuality in relationships and sensitivity to society, ecology and human cultures.

God created a wholesome and pleasing universe of beings. In Africa, creation myths of 'The Beginning', whether set in pastoral or agricultural communities, manifest a relationship of sufficiency of nature for human life and a relatively closer rapport between God, humans and the rest of nature. Creation stories do not speak of uniformity. There is differentiation, but it was all part of what was pleasant until the narrators took a closer look at life as it is actually lived. Why death, why disease, why drought, why the hierarchy in human relations, why the variety of relationships between humans and the rest of creation? And the biggest 'why' of all: 'Why does God seem to be absent at the most critical times?'

Here begins the women's consciousness of the injustice of telling creation stories that make the divine source of life into a male who is good and does what is good, and femaleness as an opposing principle that destroys God's goodness, typically causing the felt distance between God and humanity. In African mythology, to balance the allegation that it was a woman who caused God to move away from human habitation, there is also a myth which claims that it was the stubbornness of a man who accidentally discovered fire which caused God to move away. In addition, there are many folktales in which indigent men are given cities by benevolent old women. These stories end with the men losing everything and returning to the original state of poverty because they were disobedient to the covenant with the donor of the good estate. These alternative myths are liberative in African theology. In the alternative theological myths from Africa, God the Supreme Being and ultimate origin of all that exists, defies the gender category. Most of Africa has no images of God, so where there are no gender-specific pronouns it has been insisted that God is supra-gender. It is also asserted that the God that created males created females, gave both the same spirit, and called both human. What is central to our humanity, therefore, is that both female and male are akin to God, having received the same divine spirit. Gender does not define our worthiness, since it is not present in God. For this reason in the theological writings of African women, the gender of God plays a marginal role.

Musimbi Kanyoro, one of the few who have taken this factor seriously, has this to say:

> To engage in theological dialogue with gender issues means to attempt to see how the perception of gender in society has affected our understanding of God, the Scriptures, the teaching and the practice of the church, and our relationship as men and women with one another (Kanyoro 1997: 63).

In the Christian heritage, the traditional imagery that makes Yahweh male has played havoc with both our theology and our ethics. That our necessarily anthropomorphic language may be leading us to create God in our image and God's will in terms of the norms of the status quo that suits the powers that be, is yet to be seriously considered a part of the theological agenda of African theologians, and the women who see it as such hesitate to make it a central consideration. They take refuge in the many non-gender specific names and attributes of God in their traditions.

We cannot ignore the fact that while there are many non-gender specific and functional names of God, there are specific male appellations and other references to God that attribute gender, some male, others female. In the end, most African women and men would say that the gender of God is irrelevant to their theology and spirituality. Attributes said to be feminine and others said to be masculine are all applied to God. While there is specifically male and specifically female imagery of the Source Being to be found in Africa, under the influence of Christianity and Islam a patriarchal God has been enthroned, in whose name women who pray to God as 'God our Mother' are victimized. Women struggle to understand God, eliciting meaning from the many models of conceiving God, and with their relation—if any— to the maleness of the males of the human species in human societies. It is for these reasons that creation narratives, both biblical and African, have featured extensively in African women's theology.

Many of the mythological sources as well as the folktales are, for the main part, disempowering to women. Nevertheless, there is enough in them to demonstrate that in the African worldview, evil is perpetrated in the realm of the spirit by both human beings and aggrieved spirits. It is the use of power in a negative and life-denying or death-promoting manner. In the Yoruba belief, it is *aiye*, which Idowu defines as 'the concentration of evil power in the world'. This is what is often attributed to women. There is also *ashe*, 'the personality force by which one impresses one's authority or will effectively upon another or upon a situation'. All human beings possess both sorts of spiritual power. The popular belief, however, is that women are more often into *aiye* than men. What this means in practice is that women are more often accused of using *aiye* as in witchcraft. On the other hand women may not use *ashe* except to secure the good of the community.

When women are hedged in with so much ritual and so many taboos that they have to live carefully in order not to unleash *aiye* on their family, kin and community, women theologians cannot help but examine the concept of evil and its origin in their attempt to talk about God and from God. They have to discern what is of God. There are many blood and purity regulations in Africa's religio-culture that are similar to biblical injunctions. This has meant that women ask to know whether these are of God, and if so, whether there is a word from God for today's world on the concerns behind these taboos? Women are also the target of many rituals and intercessory prayers, mostly for fertility. Women ask 'what does God expect of humanity as we "increase and multiply and fill the earth"?' Hence fruitfulness and abundance are themes that are related to God, the bountiful giver of all that is good. This is attested to by prayers in African Religion. The myths about difficult births, multiple births, infant mortality and several stressful conditions for which women are blamed and victimized are the subjects of theological reflection for women. Does God demand that women undergo purification after child birth or is this a cultural practice that arises from fear of the mystery of new life? What does new birth, the continual renewal of the human community, say about God?

The Image of God

The God-talk emanating from the discussion of myths of origins needs to have women's perspectives firmly included, hence women's study of the religio-culture of Africa. That God is the source of life and being is a factor that all religious people avow. In African Religion we find God who is caring and compassionate, but God does have the power to punish injustice. We threaten bullies and exploiters with 'God will pay you back'. We believe that God has the power to enable us to overcome the difficulties that we meet in life and that the ultimate outcome of all belongs to God. 'If God has not killed you, no human being can cause your death'. This God is a helper of all creation. This is the common heritage of Africans, women and men. The challenge to women's theological discourse is the nature of God and how to come to statements about God that are empowering to women.

From myths and other folktalk—that is, maxims, proverbs and folktales—we find God depicted not only as source of all life, but also as its sustainer and the controller of human evolution. We come from God and we go back to God. In between we live our lives in the presence of God, so life is definitely theocentric. God occupies a side of the triangle of relations that describes the structure of African Religion.[2] Humans, in the palpable dimension, and spirits, in the 'world in between', are all derived from, linked to and accountable to God. In the dimension of the spirits are those related to the whole cosmos as of other principles experienced by humans. We also have in this dimension the spirits of humans who once shared our space as humans. The spirits, commonly designated 'ancestors', continue to interact with us even as they continue to relate to God. It is believed that God sends them back to us as newborn babes. The theology, then, is one that proposes one divine source of all being.

In this scheme the image of God is that of the unique source to which we are bound as humans and to whom we owe the responsibility to account for the state of the environment in which we have been placed. All of this presents a picture of the unity of the cosmos and of life as a circle of relationships involving the natural and the supernatural. There is, therefore, no need to divide life into sacred and secular. Religion permeates all life. This makes prayer a central and regular part of life in Africa, thus giving God the image of one who is close to the human community, who listens to us, and gets involved in our daily lives. God is imaged as the one who holds the cosmos together in unity.

That this is God's world, God's realm and sphere of influence has led to women's affirmation of equality before God and in the human community. Equal worth and joint responsibility are presented by women as deriving from God who makes us all human. It is to make this operative that women theologians awaken the determination to co-operate in obedience to God rather than to men. God expects this of all humans. Anything else is idolatry. God-talk in African Religion links who God is to who humans are. We affirm boldly, 'God does not die: in consequence, neither do I.' Our immortality is guaranteed by the nature of God. As these multiple images of God are alive among Africans, the

2.   The three sides of the triangle of relations are God; other spirit beings; physical beings including humans.

naming of God by female qualities is in theory theologically correct. But, in actual fact, among African Christians this is yet to become the practice. African women theologians are therefore very tentative about naming God as both inclusive of female and male, and above gender and sexuality. It has been left as an area of low priority, though a few attempts do exist.

Creation and Inter-relatedness

God, the unique source of all creation, makes all that exists sacred. In African Religion, God is present to and in more than human beings. Creation and other beings are in the ambit of God. This theocentrism is the beginning of women's ecotheology. Most African women live close to nature; we are in touch with our rural economies and cultures and, therefore, with the ethic and spirituality of our primal religion which requires us to be sensitive to both the visible and the invisible world as being the domain of God. It is this fact that has been vitalized to strengthen the factor of inter-relatedness. Discussions of this have taken the form of examination of God's hospitality and human response. The networks of relationships—human and the rest of nature, between genders, among ages and races and ethnic groups—are all reviewed from within a creation perspective before any other considerations are pursued. Denise Ackermann and Tahira Joyner of South Africa have written about the strain of anthropocentric attitudes that seriously devalue women and nature (Ackermann and Joyner 1996). In the same anthology Mutasa Nyajeka observes how in Shona religion all creation in relation to the Creator is of equal status and worth (Nyajeka 1996). This illustrates African Religion's principles of oneness and egalitarianism as including the rest of creation.

In African women's theology, hospitality is a word that generates the themes of caring, providing, helping, sharing and 'ministering' to the needs of others and most often the concept of 'mothering' (Kanyoro 1996b). Women experience several traditional practices of hospitality that are accompanied by risk of disease and violence, not to mention economic strains. The servant role of women and the expected servility and self-abasement has stimulated examination of the theology of the cross and of sacrifice. At a 1996 consultation in Douala, the following biblical episodes formed the basis of theological reflection on hospitality. Women's experience of domestic hospitality is that of Sarah, a situation in which they work and the men take the credit (Gen. 18.1-15). Rebekah's hospitality to the servant of Isaac (Gen. 24.15-27) is traditional to Africa. The story of the anonymous Nigerian woman who gave Mungo Park, the explorer, a drink and took him in and fed him, is typical of the African hospitality that continues to sustain African refugees where no formal structures exist to institutionalize them. Reciprocal hospitality was affirmed in the relations between Elisha and the Shunemite widow (2 Kgs 4.8-37). To illustrate the exploitation of women in men's hospitality to men, African women theologians recall Abraham passing Sarah off as his sister; Lot offering his virgin daughters in order to save his male guests (Gen. 19.1-8) and the horrible murder of the 'Levite's Concubine' (Judg. 19.22-30).

From these and several other biblical events—like the negotiations around the rape of Dinah, the double standards implied in the story of Tamar wife of Er; the socialization that pushed the other Tamar and Ruth to offer themselves to men of their husbands' patrilineage—women debate the limits of hospitality. On the other hand, Deut. 22.13-30, which stipulates that rape is an unacceptable behavior, was a source of strength, while the Greek Bible's examples and admonitions not to neglect hospitality (Heb. 13.1-3) enabled discussions on the nature of the hospitality of God to creation and the hospitality God expects from human beings. For, as African Religion enjoins, as God is so we should be. Papers from The Circle conference in Nairobi in 1996 show a shift of emphasis towards God's hospitality as a paradigm for human hospitality.

The indescribable provision for the sustenance of life, which God has made, constitutes for theology a challenge to articulate faith with regard to the natural resources and the ecological interdependence. The issue is the crafting of an appropriate theology of creation to counter environmental degradation. Human stewardship of creation does not seem strong enough to counteract ignorance, poverty and the corrupting greed that afflict many in Africa. In the face of this, women call attention to the inter-relationship of all creation. Another approach is to point to the indiscriminate provision for the sustenance of all life and to call on humans to do the same. In this respect women see themselves as highlighting the example of Mary the mother of Jesus who received the Christ-child even under culturally unacceptable conditions.

God's hospitality to humanity is defined at times as 'mothering'. God nurtures and mentors as a compassionate mother. Mothering, as a model of godlikeness, has been explored by several African women including myself (see Ekeya 1994). Another approach to the subject of God, women and motherhood or mothering is explored by Rosemary Edet (1991). While these women present biological motherhood and female-ness as principles included in the image of God, I emphasize 'mothering' as a quality of relating which is found in God and is expected not only of women but of men and women because we are beings created in the image of God.

This world that God has generously offered all of creation is also our home and responsibility as men and women. But a Chewa (Malawian) creation myth reminds us that God gave woman the responsibility to nurture her children (that is, men), into apologizing when they have wronged another. This is interpreted to signify that women are to see to the cultivating of life-enhancing relationships in the human community. Women are also called by God to see to it that all humanity lives in harmony with all other creatures and to honor her, that is, God. For when God, Namalenga the mother, visits humanity, she descends on women and gives them the message for all. The image of the 'mothering God' is thereby firmly lodged in the souls of many in Africa. It is also through God the mother that all find their inter-relationship.

Theo-Logos

Theology, God-talk, is about God, the divine, the sacred. Hence, all that is, is related to this unique source of being. Derived from this is the strong focus on contextual studies. The study of African Religion, the sociopolitical, economic and cultural experiences are all relevant to the sacred. Rachel Tetteh reminds us that:

> If theology hinges on human thinking and application of the revelation of God, and how that revelation affects us as human beings, then theology needs to be applied in all everyday activities (Tetteh 1997: 61).

Then she names several religio-cultural practices on which she proceeds to reflect theologically. As in other African women's reflections, her theology is about putting things right under divine guidance; it is empowering the marginalized to live out their faith. African women appeal to justice in the Bible when they speak out on economy, power, empowerment and women's participation in justice-making.

Affirming the Bible as a source for God-word brings women into the arena of biblical hermeneutics. In addition, African women have to ask:

'Whose voice is the voice of the ancestors, the voice of tradition?' and 'Where is the voice for today coming from?'. They raise a question on the authority that keeps religious rites, rituals and demands in place even where they are dehumanizing and do not seem to confer any obvious benefit on the subject/object. With the notion and practice of globalization has come the cultural revival of oppressed and marginalized peoples. Women ask, 'By what criteria does one opt for continuation or work for change?'. Revival of oppressed traditions brings with it the removal of traditional religious devotion, the cultural hermeneutics. African women theologians seek a way to the word that God speaks through and about the practice of religion.

Flowing from contextual studies is the realization that in spite of the vaunted adherence to religion attributed to Africans, much needs to be transformed if that picture is to remain true in deed and not simply in forms of outward religiosity. Putting things right is discussed with a focus on women's lives, but with a view to pointing to a prophetic word on the vision of a household of God where righteousness prevails. What has become a source of strength is discerning and interpreting the presence of the divine, God, Nyame, Allah, Yahweh. The presence of 'the presence', however you name it, is what enables our interpretation of experience, our protest against injustice and our honoring of our humanity which carries the image of the divine in us. The theology of the total depravity of humanity is not in African Religion and has not taken root among African women even though certain types of Christian theology insist on it. African women see God at work and they recognize humans who collaborate with this work.

Source, Reason and End of Life

Margaret Umeagudosu writes, 'God to most Africans is beyond morality, that is, capable of good and evil, and can wreak vengeance on both the guilty humans and spirits' (Umeagudosu 1997: 12). In West Africa where slogans on vehicles and storefronts depict people's rottenness in religion, sayings such as 'only God Knows' or 'The end is in God's Head/Hands' are very common. In saying this, people leave the outcome of human endeavors in the hands of God, assured that the divine plan cannot but be for the ultimate *alafia* of the whole creation. Speaking of God as source, reason and end of life has led women to examine more closely the concepts of grace and compassion. The eschatology of

African women's theology is firmly lodged in the God of life, whose end is to defeat death and enthrone life forever. It is for this reason that most of the statements about God in this theology are made in the context of liberation and transformation.

African women who read the Bible with a critical eye discover in it the Triune God as liberator of the oppressed, the rescuer of the marginalized and all who live daily in the throes of pain, uncertainty and deprivation. Added to this is the fact that in African Religion, God is always present in human affairs, as in the rest of creation, as judge, healer and the one who takes the side of the weak and the vulnerable, as in the affirmation 'God drives the flies off the body of the tail-less animal'. With the collaborative evidence from biblical stories, women in theology have appropriated a liberation motif together with the 'image of God' motif to stake a claim to freedom from oppression, to full humanity and full membership in the 'household of God' and a place in 'the great economy of God', in which all are worthy. They hold on to the faith that Yahweh is the God of the oppressed who are to live as God's people, and claim the power of God that accords with the situation from which they need to be liberated. God is adequate for all occasions and against holding creation in bondage.

God plays the part of kin, a member of the community and reclaims that which has been lost and takes care of orphans and widows. As many women often feel themselves in bondage or lost in the 'foreign lands' of affinal communities, the theologians see the acts of God in the Hebrew culture portrayed in the Book of Ruth as illustrative of the kinship role of God. The saving acts of God in African Religion and in the Hebrew Bible are often worked into those of God in Christ in the Greek Testament and into the anthropology, for nobody is a nobody, all being people of God. Therefore without God all is naught and one can use the Akan symbol *Gye Nyame* as the central motif for African women's theology.

Chapter Four

Jesus the Divine–Human: Christology

The word 'Christology' is not in the vocabulary of African Christian women unless they have had some formal theological education; but they all talk about Jesus, believe in Jesus, relate closely to Jesus the son of Mary and testify to what Jesus has done for them. The story that characterizes African women's Christology is not the meaning of the incarnation, nor the annunciation, the meeting of Mary and the angel, but what is usually referred to as 'the visitation'—the episode in which Mary visited Elizabeth in the anonymous Judean town in the hill country. Childbearing is central to African women's self-image, and the scene of the two women swapping pregnancy announcements is a precious one for African women. That the younger woman paid a visit to the older one to share her strange experience signifies for them the solidarity that women crave in times of crisis and in other significant moments of their lives. In this case they shared their common experience of uncommon conception. Their expected births were due to special divine intervention, just what African women pray for in their dread of the reproach that accompanies childlessness. Together, they rejoiced at God's salvation, which comes through women. As unborn speaks to unborn, God's future as discerned by women is made ready by women to be communicated among and by women to the whole community.

In this study the primary sources are my own 'christological journey', that of Bette Ekeya and the reflections of Anne Nasimiyu on women's stories of 'meetings' with Jesus. These will be augmented with statements from several other women. It will be like Mary and Elizabeth sharing stories of salvation, for in general, African theology tends to treat Christology from the stand point of soteriology. It is what responds to the quest for life and more life that African Religion pursues.

Amba's Story

Christology is a familiar word among Christian theologians and one that is quite able to stand by itself and be explicated as a theological issue and concept. What have women got to do with the concept of Christology? What do women say about Christology? Is there such a thing as women's Christology? Do the traditional statements of Christology take into account women's experiences of life? These and many others are the questions that led me to re-read the Christology I had studied and to reflect on what I had heard from pulpits. In this process of reviewing what I knew, I heard Jesus say to me, 'And you, who do you say that I am? And why are you using this technical word when it is me, Jesus of Nazareth, you encounter?'

So then, I looked again at the word *Christology*. I can recognize the word 'Christ'; The '-ology' bit comes as the second half of many long words and means the 'study of', coming from the Greek word *logos* (word or reason). Hence one could describe Christology simply as a reasoned account of what the word Christ stands for. Christology then is the church's word about The Christ. The question asked by Jesus does not go away. What do I say about The Christ? To answer this I go back to what has been said by the Church but especially to the fundamental beliefs that have led to those statements. So first I will take a brief excursus into Hebrew Scriptures and the Greek Bible, called the 'New Testament'. Next, I will look at a broad outline of what the issues were during the first five centuries of the Christian era; and before coming to what this one African woman, Amba, wishes to be said about the Christ, I shall peep into the Christology of the missionary era that created the current phase of Christianity in Africa. I begin, therefore, with the biblical account.

In the Protestant theological schema, there is a fundamental principle of revelation, which states that the golden thread running through the whole Bible is 'The Christ'. Obviously one does not intend to debate or do justice to the dictum in such a personal statement. All that can be done is to present a slide show of the meaning of 'The Christ' in the various stages of the development of the biblical materials.

The term 'The Christ', is Greek *ho christos*, meaning 'the anointed one' and is said to be used to translate the Hebrew *messiah*—the same word as in the English. In Hebrew religion and culture, prophets, priests and kings were anointed, as were the sick, the dying and the dead. In their struggle to survive as a culturally and materially insignificant and martially impotent nation among the powerful ones of the Fertile Crescent, the Hebrews hankered after the return of the one illustrious king they produced, David. Buffeted around by more powerful nations, the People of Israel were sustained by the faith that, in due course, Yahweh will send them a Ruler like David, an anointed one, a Messiah. This hope was very much alive right into the period of the Roman colonization of Palestine.

Before then, with the Babylonian occupation, apocalyptic literature such as the book of Daniel introduced the figure of the human-being who will descend from the clouds with angels to inaugurate a new era of God's Reign. These two figures—'the anointed one' and 'the human one from above'—became the Christian paradigms for the explanation of who Jesus of Nazareth was. Certainly, he was a man from Nazareth, but just as surely he was not like any of the other men of Nazareth. 'Who is this that the winds and the seas obey?', asked his immediate companions. There are several other names used for Jesus: Son of God and Lord occur quite frequently, but the Letter to the Hebrews adds that of High Priest.

Beginning from the first two centuries of the Christian era, parts of which we have in the New Testament, the figure of the Christ as Lord was the most prominent. Jesus is Lord, not Caesar, and that brought persecution to the early believers. As Christianity became more and more fashionable with the inauguration of the Constantinian period, Christ the Glorious King gained ascendancy. The most crucial struggles for the interpretation of who Jesus was ceased to be what he was in relation to the religious and political powers of the age, but rather who he was in view of Greek philosophy (a taste of which we get in John's prologue on the Logos of God in the Fourth Gospel) and Hebrew monotheism. Hence the debates that led to the Niceno-Constantinopolitan Creed in which we state what we believe about Jesus the Christ even to this day. Having stated the Christ-events we profess our faith in Jesus the Christ as God and Human, God enfleshed (incarnated) as human, so that we might come a little closer to understanding both divinity and humanity. The debates were endless and several emphases developed in this attempt to state who the Christ is in his nature as divine–human. Later Christologies, however, followed the Pauline line of approaching the issue from the angle of soteriology—what Christians say about salvation. Christology was moving from attempts at ontological statements towards being relevant to the world of believers. The answer to the question 'Who am I' was being answered, 'You are the Savior'. Since one is always saved from something in order that a new life might emerge, the christological discussions moved to the question 'Saved from what?' It is with this contextualized Christology that I cast my lot. It is the struggles of the early Christians that empower each generation; and it is for each place to state who the Christ is for them.

Rooted in the Hebrew Scriptures and the Jewish understanding of how God deals with persons and peoples, salvation accrued to itself a variety of connotations. An example is evident in the concept of salvation from sin, where sin meant alienation from God and from other human beings. Salvation was seen as liberation from oppressive forces, be they natural and political, sociological and religious. In positive terms, salvation was related to a new beginning, a new life and the full experience of the reign of God. Jesus, the Christ was the agent of it all. His followers began to see his own life as a liberated and liberating one, and to tell of the annunciation of his birth to show how oppressive cultures are set aside in order to bring in the reign of God.

The events of Jesus' life, his solidarity with the poor and the marginalized, his championing of the cause of what is life-giving and his obedience and dependence upon God who alone has life, began to take center stage in the accounts of the preached Christ. That story saw suffering, sacrifice and the Cross, as salvific. The Christ is the one who suffers so that humanity might have the fullness of life intended for them by God. These early efforts have provided road marks for getting on with walking with Jesus. But the Western missionary enterprise in Africa inaugurated a Christology that took no account of Africa's realities beyond the existence of numerous divinities and ancestral spirits. The emphasis, therefore, was Jesus as the only way to God. Jesus, the mediator and high priest, has been consistently preached in the Western churches in Africa, that is, in Roman Catholic and churches of the Reformation.

Meanwhile, Africa kept Africa's realities and fears, and the African Instituted Churches have picked up the fears and have successfully transmitted the faith in a Victorious Christ, Christ the conqueror and the annuller of the powers of Satan (a character created by Christianity), and all the witches and evil spirits who are Satan's agents and emissaries. Since the 1980s a new form of Christianity that dispenses salvation through the total alienation of Africans from African culture and the instrumentalization of the gospel for material prosperity is taking over the Christian scene. The name of Jesus is peddled by hundreds of Gospel singers and fast energetic liturgies. None of these Christologies have anything special to say to women or from women except that women's prayers and songs tell who the Christ is for them.

The Christ whom African women worship, honor and depend on is the Victorious Christ: knowing that evil is a reality, there is a lot that we bring upon ourselves—in my language this is *mmusu*. But there is also a lot of *Esian* evil that we encounter because of the *mmusu* of others, or from sources we do not understand. It is especially for *Esian* that we need the power of Jesus. Death and life-denying forces are the experience of women and so Christ who countered their powers and gave back the widow of Nain's child to her, is the African woman's Christ (Oduyoye 1989a).

This has been Amba's story. The story of a woman whose concern has been how to make the story of Jesus the context in which African women can read their lives. There are several images of the Christ that are dear to African women and which will be illustrated below. They are also just as 'subjective' but we cannot tell them all. The christological statements of African women have to be heard with the following in mind:

> It is rather difficult for me to write an article on Christology from an objective, that is, from an academically theological point of view, for the simple reason that the question as to who and what Christ is, has been a most subjective and absorbing problem for me. My experience and understanding of the person, role and significance of Christ, has been that of a woman on the underside (Ekeya 1988: 17).

Christ is the liberator from the burden of disease and from taboos that restrict women's participation in their communities. The triple burdens of racism, poverty and marginalization are countered by claims that Christ liberates from oppressive cultures. They see the Christ figure as the one who voluntarily lived a life that was life-giving for others and even died for the same. Following Jesus, African women approve of costly sacrifice but they insist it must be voluntary and it must be the duty of both men and women. In a continent and church that does not allow much visibility for women it is necessary that we hear the story of women who write from that location, so we hear excerpts from Bette Ekeya's 'A Christology from the Underside' (1988), on Christ and the single woman or unmarried mother.

Bette's Story

Bette writes from the standpoint of the underside, which she describes as 'any oppressive factor or experience of life which prevents persons from responding successfully to the challenge of developing their fullest humanity'. She specifies further that the underside she is writing from 'is that age-long powerlessness which women have lived with and learned to assimilate as a necessary aspect of being woman in a world defined by men'. This context of powerlessness, she says, has condemned women to positions of subservience. Bette sees subservience and subjugation as what has prevented women from 'fully apprehending the truly good news that Jesus Christ's coming has brought especially for women'. Her story is based on the experience of what she calls 'a new class of African women who are emerging: the single or unmarried mothers'.

Bette describes the African woman in traditional Africa as an intensely practical theologian, living her faith in God within her traditional religious beliefs, cultural taboos and practices. Then came the Christian missions who condemned all this and the African woman who abandoned her rituals in favor of Christianity. Now a vacuum has been created in the lives of the women because it 'is taking a long time for the Christ of the Gospels to become incarnate in the life of the African woman'. Bette describes the Christ of the missionaries as 'a rather forbidding figure…and an exacting judge'. Through preaching she was taught 'a Christ who excluded women from intimate participation in divine mysteries, who seemed to demand of them that they be subjugated, subservient and forever innocent and frozen in religious adolescence'. The Christ of damnation was enthroned in the place of the Christ of liberation.

African women who turned to the African Instituted Churches (AICs) found the hidden Christ of the 'Western Churches'. In the AICs they found the 'victorious Christ'. They discovered Christ's 'power to heal, willingness to suffer with those who suffer, and His joy of liberation.' They found the Christ who 'declared that He had come to set the captives free, to give sight to the blind, wholeness to the lame and to proclaim good news to the poor.' Women now identify with a Christ 'who does not lay unnecessary burdens on their already burdened lives, but one whose power and victory over the powers of darkness they can experience and testify to.' Bette has drawn all this from the lived experiences of actual women whose stories she tells in this article and whose

understanding and experience of Christ she shares with us. Bette concludes: 'It is only fair that (single mothers and others whom the Church
excludes) should be enabled to see in Jesus Christ the friend who long
ago entrusted one of their kind with the all important mission of
announcing the Resurrection to his brothers.' African women indeed do
see such a friend in Jesus and they sing in affirmation: 'When we are
carrying burdens that bend our backs, who but Jesus helps us set them
down?'

The Story of Jesus who Saves

In a continent where physical suffering seems endemic, a suffering
Christ is a most attractive figure, for that Christ can be a companion. To
the African mind, however, all suffering has to be like birth pangs: it has
to lead to a birth, it has to lead to a new beginning, so women create for
themselves a Jesus who will mid-wife the birth of the new. In a continent where hunger, thirst and homelessness are the continuous experience of millions, Jesus of Nazareth is a comrade. But women know that
although Jesus took on hunger voluntarily, he never accepted deprivation as the destiny of humanity; rather he demonstrated that suffering is
not in the plan of God, hence the emphasis of the victorious Christ in
African women's spirituality. The back-drop of this Christology shows
the world structures and human experiments that are affecting Africans
adversely—cut the trees in Brazil and the drought intensifies in the
Sahel. So women theologians, in reflecting on the meaning of Jesus in
their lives, do not evade the necessity to explore socio-political-econo-
mic analysis. They do this in both national and global contexts, but most
importantly, they do it from their own daily lives as women in community. In this they are doing what Jesus did:

> In his [Jesus'] witness here on earth, Jesus visited all the towns and villages
> and saw with his own eyes the problems facing the people. He saw
> poverty, the inequality, the religious and economic oppression, the un-
> employment, the depression, the physically ill and the socially unclean.
> His heart was filled with pity. In his witness Jesus told people: 'the
> time is fulfilled, and the kingdom of God has come near; repent and
> believe in the good news' (Kanyoro 1996a [unpublished]).

Christology, for African women, is the story of Jesus who saves, the one
who not only announces, but also brings and lives good news.

The Annunciation speaks of God's liberative work in history, but it is
a history that singles out women to be God's agents of salvation. In

African women's theology, it is through the living and telling of Jesus who saves, that Christology is to be discerned. Re-telling the Jesus story has unveiled aspects of the gospel which speak to women and which they share with and beyond their faith community. The solidarity of Joseph with Mary, his love and respect for her, his sensitivity to God at work through a woman and his willingness to go against the norms of the culture in order to do the will of God, reflects the approach of Jesus and gives women a handle for discerning God at work and the courage to be at work with God. The Magnificat is a cardinal hermeneutical key for African women's Christology. Their Christology, like the testimonies of Elizabeth and Mary, are anchored on real life experiences.

Terese Souga writes: 'Christology cannot be formulated without taking into account women and their place in Church and society' (Souga 1988: 29). In this joint work by two Cameroonians, there is a general affirmation of African men's Christology, with a caution that it is not adequate because it does not take account of women's experience (Souga 1988: 29). For these women, Christology is not a discourse but a relationship between Jesus and women that leads them to discover for themselves that Jesus reveals God. Louise Tappa writes: 'To work out the full meaning of the Christ-event for humankind' has been the aim of African Christologies. This has meant that women contemplate and thank Jesus in relation to their situation and their praxis. Her Christology, she says, puts more emphasis on the praxis of Jesus who brings women 'full liberation to enable women's self affirmation' (Tappa 1988). A poem, *My Name is Woman*, by Rachel Etrue Tetteh in which she describes her faith journey, is typical of the testimonies that women give of their life in Christ. In part it reads:

> I heard of the Good News, now ours
> Requiring men and women to hear, read and spread
> The Gospel of what Jesus had done for humanity…
> His ministry included women freed to make a choice
> to follow Christ whose love
> includes all men and women…
> Daughters of Africa Arise (Tetteh 1990a: 229).

'Freed to choose' could be the organizing principle for most of what African women say about their encounter with Jesus. Jesus is the antidote to their ascribed positions in church and society, the cultural contexts in which they experience the Christ in their lives.

Jesus of African Women

Teresa Hinga in *The Will to Arise* writes on 'Jesus Christ and the Liberation of Women', outlining some of the cultural contexts that have influenced the focus of Christology on liberation. She points out however that in the AICs, 'patronized mostly by women', there is a 'pneumatic Christology' at work which 'empowers women to be less inhibited and muted'. The Spirit of Christ is at work here, making Christ the 'voice of the voiceless, the power of the powerless'. Also in these churches the prophetic role of Jesus as 'champion of the cause of the voiceless and the vindicator of the marginalised in society' is particularly attractive to women (Hinga 1992: 191). Earlier, Oduyoye had offered a view on Christology under the title 'Jesus Saves' in her *Hearing and Knowing* (Oduyoye 1986: 97-108). Observing the constant use of the affirmation 'Jesus saves', Oduyoye suggests that in a multireligious community the meaning of 'Jesus saves' 'should not be a meta-physical analysis of what it means to be truly God and truly human but rather the christological quest of our times'. The questions she brings to Christology are related to the meaning of the Christ-event in view of the challenges of racism, sexism and other contexts including the multireligious in which we profess Christ.[1]

A collection of essays on Christology features three women, namely, Judith Bahemuka, Hannah Kinoti and Anne Nasimiyu (Mugambi and Magesa 1989; Oduyoye 1986: 97-108). All these theologies derive from experience of life in Africa. Bahemuka, however, attempts to unveil the 'Hidden Christ in African Religion', taking seriously Idowu's assertion that we cannot ignore the African Religion in seeking to articulate Christology, if we believe that the God of our creation is the same as the God of our redemption (Idowu 1975: 25; cf. Oduyoye 1986: 75). The theme of Jesus through African idioms has been eloquently demonstrated in *Jesus of the Deep Forest*, the prayers and praises of Efua Kuma, a Ghanaian farmer, mid-wife and a member of an AIC (Kuma 1980). From these three women we retrieve a Christology of Jesus the wonder worker, portrayed in imagery found in African Religion. Jesus was the one who came into the burning furnace to be near us and to walk with us (Dan. 3.25). Jesus is the place of rest. By utilizing imagery from her

---

1. See Oduyoye (1984), where this concern is expressed.

Akan worldview, Efua Kuma portrays dramatically the paradigm shift that Jesus has introduced into the beliefs about who God is, which have become empowering for her as a woman.

Amoah and Oduyoye (1988) reflect on the Christ as portrayed by African women who see the Christ of Christian Scriptures and tradition as one who has made Africa's business his business. They demonstrate women's close walk with Jesus from Efua Kuma. For many women who go to church, Christ the Word comes as a story. Increasingly, Jesus comes to Africans through the lyrics of 'Gospel Singers' many of whom in Ghana are women. Efua Kuma is the precursor of women's written poetry about Jesus in Ghana. Fanti lyrics and Christian extemporary prayers—yet to be recorded—bear the prayers and praises of women directed to Jesus, and which tell us who they affirm the Christ to be. The language is graphic and moving. Efua Kuma calls to Jesus:

> Yesu who has received the poor and makes us honorable our exceedingly wise friend, we depend on you as the tongue depends on the jaw...You are the rock. We hide under you, the great bush with cooling shades, the giant tree who enables the climbers to see the heavens (Kuma 1980: 5).

And women from Northern Nigeria join the chorus 'Jesus the rock, the living rock, I find in thee my resting place, Jesus the living rock'. From these expressions women theologians, like Kinoti, underline the faith of women in Jesus who is real and satisfies any circumstances. Women understand what it means in practice to say that with Jesus one can live the victorious life. Anne Nasimiyu describes Christology 'as a place where we envision the redemption from sin and evil. It is a symbol which encompasses our vision of our authentic humanity and the ful-filled hopes of all human persons' (1991: 70). Recognizing the oppres-sive context out of which she writes, she observes that African women have learnt tolerance, and that they fatalistically accept the given con-ditions. When she interviewed some women with the question 'Who is Jesus to you?' she got several images including 'Jesus is my strength, savior, hope, model, helper, teacher, my everything and my God'. 'Jesus is kind and generous and shares in my sorrows when I am in trouble'. So far there has never been a meeting of The Circle without someone raising the hymn 'What a friend we have in Jesus'. They all draw great strength from the relationship of Jesus and women in the Gospels.

Christological Reflections

Reflecting on all this Nasimiyu comes to the following findings: Christology has to respond to the whole of life. In African women's faith expressions we come into contact with a Christology that derives from experience. 'African Christian women need a Christ who relates to God. The God who can be reached through the spirits and the "Living dead" or direct intercession…this God the Christ is the one who takes on the conditions of African women: conditions of weakness, misery, injustice and oppression'. African women's Christology, as Nasimiyu portrays it, unveils the Christ who empowers women to reject androcentric culture, the one who comes to heal our broken communities, and who empowers and enables the downtrodden to realize their dignity and worth as persons (a summary of Nasimiyu 1989: 124-31).[2] She finds a variety of Christologies from women's witness to Jesus. There are several well-known christological models to be discerned from women's stories: eschatological, anthropological, liberational and cosmological. Nasimiyu's summaries of these types are reflected below.

In the eschatological, Jesus is experienced as 'sent by God to an alienated world where the presence of God takes the shape of the crucified one'. This is the Jesus who suffers and dies, but is ultimately victorious over death. This model attempts to respond to the question 'Why does one who is perfect and righteous have to suffer and to die, the death of a criminal?' It points to the resurrection, 'the ultimate victory over this world's alienating forces…and opens a future for a new humanity'. Nasimiyu discerns from this that women accept the teaching that Christ takes on our suffering, so we are invited to take on and 'participate in the restoration of harmony, equality and inclusiveness in all human relationships, in the family, society and Church'.

On the anthropological model she writes: 'God calls us in Christ to a life-style that is dedicated to the love of neighbor and to a life which puts others first and gives them life.' She describes Jesus as the mother, the nurturer of life, especially that of the weak. This reflects, accurately, the African women's primary experience of themselves in relation to others as mothers. But Nasimiyu does not neglect to point out that Jesus

---

2. Nasimiyu concludes that if one wishes to theorize about women's Christology one could find several well-known models. But that would not be the voices of African women.

recognized women as responsible persons and took them seriously (Lk. 8.1-3; 11.27-28). She adds: 'Today Jesus would have insisted on women being also theological teachers, catechists, biblical interpreters, counselors... (and as persons) called to restore the church and humanity to the initial inclusive, holistic and mutual relationships between women and men.'

On the liberational model, Christ is the liberator. Nasimiyu declares that 'Jesus asks African women not to accept their hardships and pain fatalistically but to work at eliminating the suffering and creating a better place for all.' Looked at it from this stand point, she sees women's struggles becoming 'God's struggles... It is then Jesus who suffers in them and their works to give birth to new and better human relationships.' Marie Assaad commenting on Lk. 1.26-45 sees in the passage God's reversing of what we say is the 'natural order'. God reverses all we take as the natural order of this world and is still asking us today to reverse this order (Assaad 1986: 25-27). The liberation that Christ brings covers all creation: thus in the cosmological model, Christ restores the whole cosmos (Rom. 8; 20–23). The groaning creation, as in the pain of childbirth, is to reconcile all things to God. She adds: 'Jesus of the gospels was sensitive to beauty of lilies, birth, beautiful weddings, beauty of a human body without disease. So Jesus is right with us as we heal, restoring nature, individuals and communities.'

In all these studies of Jesus and women in the Gospels, African women see the initiative and participation of women as important. Mary's saying 'Yes' to God; the women going to the tomb; the woman who decided to break the rules in Mk 5.25-29; the Samaritan woman— all relate Christology to women's lives. Grace Eneme ends her reflection on 'Living Stones' with:

> Sisters, power has been given to us by God. By the world's standards it can never be given to us. We have to struggle for it grab it. So gird up your loins. Christ our Liberator is our captain—that is the empowerment that comes from African women's companionship with Jesus (Eneme 1986: 32).

We observe that African women's Christology derives directly from the Gospels highlighting women's presence in the life and teaching of Jesus. The cultural hermeneutic out of which they reflect, enables them to see the ambiguities of the Jesus model as culture-coded and therefore open to transformation. The focus is on liberating the humanity of women and others whom society counts for nothing. The divine disposition is recognized by women in the Gospels, as evident in the lives of Mary, Martha and the Samaritan woman. In the Christology of African women we find Jesus the compassionate one.

The Language of Christology

In this survey we encounter the central theme of Jesus, the suffering messiah, whose nature and work is to save, for suffering and struggle are the contexts of this Christology. Christology is not meant to analyze the nature of Christ, but to identify saving acts and to cling in hope of liberation. Secondly, it is to celebrate the victories over domination and death and to attribute these to Jesus rather than to any other power. Amoah and Oduyoye (1988) focus on the victorious Christ who liberates from disease and ostracism, the child of a woman who has become the friend of women, a caring and compassionate nurturer of all. Jesus is the servant, who washes his disciples' feet, reflecting the spirituality of women's service. Jesus, the sacrificial lamb of God, points out to women the need for living sacrifice in the human community. Jesus, who breaks down barriers between God and us by forgiving our sins, also calls us to a ministry of reconciliation. In Christ all things hold together, giving back to women the integrity of their humanity. The figure of Jesus enables African women to see the Christ in the refugee. What African women's Jesus reminds us of, is that traditional Christian Christology derives from the varieties of experiences of the first followers of Jesus. African women continue this tradition. It is in the process of seeking resources from Christianity to deal with the life-denying and life-threatening contexts of Africa, that Christian women turn to Jesus. In Jesus they find resources to transform the obstacles and suffering they meet. That is why their songs are full of acknowledgment of Jesus who helps them lay down their burdens. They find examples from Scripture of Jesus as breaking the chains and the burdens of poverty, disease and exploitation. The burdens that arise from African culture are carried to Jesus as they appropriate the promises of the annunciation.

The factor of the incarnation in Christology is taken for granted. It is an area where faith accepts without plumbing the depth of meaning, admitting our limited access to knowledge of what we call reality. Jesus is a child of God *par excellence* and that is enough. Jesus is the 'man of Nazareth' who lived the life of God in the limited space of our human context. It is thus that African women appropriate Jesus as the 'anointed one of God' the Messiah. It is important for all Africans, but especially women, that this person, born in someone else's backyard, has lived the life of God on earth and continues to accompany all in similar circumstances to live their full humanity so that they too might reflect the God in whose image they are created. It was important to believe that Jesus is the anointed one of God, empowered and sent by God to show humanity what it means to live fully the image in which we are made. Living fully has come to mean resisting oppression, transforming potential death into life and believing that the resurrection happens every time we defeat death and begin a new life. This is the good news and the good experiences realized or hoped for, that give African women joy in Jesus.

Christology, therefore, takes the form of appropriating the Christ-event, seeing oneself in the daily drama that Jesus lives from cradle to cross and beyond. The circumstances of his birth are daily realities for women in Africa. Jesus' outrage against oppressive culture encourages women not to condone oppression. Jesus lived by the future of God articulated in the Magnificat, the hymn attributed to his mother. The caring compassionate healer is another strong face of Jesus that women appropriate. The lives they live need this Jesus who can exorcise the evil that torments Africa and gnaws at the womb of her daughters. Seeped in African Religion and believing in Jesus, women are able to proclaim the Jesus who breaks the chains of evil. Jesus feeds the hungry and sets free the victims of patriarchy: he is therefore the Christ for African women who know all too well the bondage of both. African women who have known Jesus, however, no longer fatalistically accept the given conditions. They refuse the Cross, as the end of their life's experience, for without the Resurrection, faith in Christ would no longer be unique. Jesus beckons them to endure the Cross, but promises fullness of life as the final outcome of their discipleship. To see Christianity grow out of the religion of Jesus the suffering servant, is what keeps African women attached to Jesus.

In the African women's Christology no distinction is made between salvation and liberation. Women are the products of Africa's holistic worldview and Jesus is experienced as responding to the totality of life. Emmanuel Lartey has described African women's Christology as 'liberation Christology', since women's aim is that Christology should be liberative as well (Lartey 1993: 82-84). Through this Christology they lay claim to the freedom they have in Jesus and are able to affirm this with the song:

I have my liberty now
Jesus has set me free now.

Liberation through Jesus is a daily reality. The editors' abstract on Bonita Bennet's contribution to *The Unquestionable Right to Be Free* (Bennet 1986) is as follows: 'only a return to the Jesus movement and to the latter's perspective on women can offer contemporary women some ideological weapons of struggle for the fight which they are inevitably engaged in'.[3] In Bennett's article we see an example of Africans' perception and experience of Jesus as standing up for women. They find in him a revolutionary stance in the patriarchal context in which he had to operate. Women take courage from the 'sensitivity and openness' of Jesus to women which enabled him to 'treat women as partners in his mission, not glorifying or belittling them' but relating to them as human beings made in the image of God. With Jesus the full humanity of women was an unquestionable fact.

---

3. Whether the women's reference to Christ should be classified as an ideology is not the issue, but it is worth noting that it is symptomatic of the inability to accept women as partners in the theological enterprise in Africa.

Chapter Five

On Being Human: A Religious Anthropology

In the beginning God created two genderless persons and gave them two bundles to keep. God told them that they were not to open the bundles until they had reached mutual understanding and friendship. As it turned out, one bundle contained female characteristics and the other, masculine. The two kept the bundles until one of them began to smell. At this point one of the persons threw out the offending bundle and opened the other. Instantly, that being became male and began to interest the partner in his sexuality. The partner, still neuter, could not respond so felt the need to go back to the creator for a resolution of the crisis. The creator gave her the gift of the characteristics of the female.

Granting the request for sexuality, God also added the knowledge of farming and home-making to the female and to the male God gave weapons so that he might protect the female. Upon their return the two discovered the differentiation and began appropriating the difference. So this is how today we are men and women.

This Bemba myth does not end with the differentiation, which was necessary for procreation. It goes on to explain the origins of the cultural role-assignments, as also God-ordained. It is this latter that women are challenging, seeing that those roles are in fact culture-conditioned and that Christianity, Westernization and modernization have produced a more complex world requiring a greater variety of skills and roles beyond the primary ones of reproduction and security. Women note that, created neuter with the possibility of differentiation, the Creator expected us to learn to appreciate, respect and value one another as primarily human. They note that as soon as the two faced their first real challenge they failed the test of mutuality and began taking unilateral actions.

Reflecting on this, and other myths, as well as on the Christ-event from their own perspective, women theologians have come to the conclusion that the Christian 'doctrine of man' does not do justice to the humanity of women. They further note that it has come into the African worldview to aggravate an already grave situation (Armstrong 1996: chs. 1–3).[1] They have, therefore, found it necessary to review this androcentric anthropology from the perspective of the Christology surveyed in the previous chapter. In *Hearing and Knowing* Oduyoye suggests that 'feminism' is a precondition for a Christian anthropology that does justice to the humanity of women. In this context she describes feminism as 'part of the whole movement geared to liberating the human community from entrenched attitudes and structures that can only operate if dichotomies and hierarchies are maintained' (Oduyoye 1986: 121). As participants in this movement, African women theologians advocate the full participation of women in all spheres of life on terms of ability and inclination, criteria that traditional anthropology undermines.

Secondly, seeing that much of African culture is patriarchal, they have found such a revisiting of human self-understanding necessary in order to find a basis for the transformation of the human relations in which it is assumed that the man takes precedence over the woman. In this regard they have resorted to the works of African women creative writers who exhibit the same concerns in order to throw light on the contemporary culture. In this chapter the writings of Buchi Emecheta will provide this back drop. Emecheta's novels portray vividly what it means to be an African woman in a patriarchal society: even the writings of some men are beginning to reflect women's voices on this situation.[2] In his *African Traditional Religion: A Definition*, E.B. Idowu says the following about Africa:

> Where she behaves herself according to prescription, and accepts an inferior position, benevolence which her 'poverty' is assured, and for this she shows herself deeply and humbly grateful. If for any reason she takes it into her head to be self-assertive and claim a footing of equality, then she

---

1.   But indeed the whole book indicates the Western Christian baggage that has arrived to augment the African woman's bundle.

2.   Oduyoye (1989c) argues that even in the matrilineal communities, patriarchal attitudes prevail and have been heightened by Westernization and Christianization that have given men powers that were not theirs in the African tradition. See also Mathabane (1994) in which he tells the lives of South African women in their own words and deals extensively with *lobola* (bride-wealth; that which goes from the groom's family to that of the bride) and its role in the patriarchal stronghold of marriage.

brings upon herself a frown; she is called names; she is persecuted openly
or by indirect means; she is helped to be divided against herself... (Idowu
1975: 77).

Idowu could have been writing about African women. Indeed my suspicion is that he is using the patriarchal ethos of the Yoruba culture to
paint this picture of 'Mother Africa'.

Helen Chukwuma, commenting on Emecheta's portrayal of the image
of African women, noted that in her novels, 'the handicap of the female
is natal' just by being born a female child (Chukwuma 1989: 3) In
Second Class Citizen (Emecheta 1974), she notes that Adah's brother had
accepted the fact that in Africa, and particularly among the Ibo, a girl
was little more than a piece of property. Another brother, this time in
The Slave Girl (Emecheta 1977), said of his sister, whom he has pawned,
'Even if she was an only daughter, she was still only a daughter' (Chukwuma 1989: 17). This assumption, that men are entitled to use women
runs through several African traditions. The male bonding is expressed
by Jessica Nakawombe from Uganda as follows: 'A son pitying his father
says of his mother; "When one's mother has aged, and her beauty faded,
then she was not worth the bride price".' In a culture that disparages the
humanity of women, the traditional Christian 'doctrine of man', that
imputes the loss of paradise to the disobedience of Eve the mother of all
humans, is certainly not one that will go unchallenged by African
women theologians who consider this culture of male entitlement
neither just nor justifiable. The search for an empowering anthropology
begins with a probe into African myths of origins, asking fresh questions
in order to untangle 'the thread which has tied women to iniquity'. In
Africa the injustice done to the humanity of the woman is linked also
with biblical narratives and their interpretations of the entrance of sin
into human affairs: hence the need to take into account both traditions.

In a Chewa (Malawi-matrilineal) myth God was driven from earth by
the wickedness of a man who accidentally created fire and would not
stop playing with it. In an Akan (Ghana-matrilineal) myth the distance
between the abode of God (the sky) and human beings was the result of
the impudence of a woman. With alternative myths available to Africans, women theologians have refused to accept the Hebrew explanation
as definitive. It is human beings, both women and men, who have
responsibility for human culture, destiny and relationship with God.
Both are truly human to the extent that they approximate God's creativity, justice and compassion and exhibit the holiness to which they are

called by God. Women insist that there is no justification for attributing human suffering to women and to use that as a reason for making women suffer and accept suffering as their lot. They reject being sacrificed and being encouraged to suffer the consequences of men's wrong decisions as well as those of their own making. If, in Christian anthropology, we need to discern the significance of suffering, we must do this without prior attribution of evil to women.

For Christian women therefore, it is more appropriate to anchor the anthropology in aspects of African Religion and of Christianity that affirm, as does Akan wisdom, that all human beings are children of God, or that all originate from the express will of God, be they male or female. Thus, Gen. 1.26, Psalm 8 and the Christ-event affirm for women the equal value of all human beings and assist in facing the challenge of difference (Ackermann 1996a). The anthropology which insists that there is something of the divine in the human culminates, for the biblical religion, in the affirmation found in Gen. 1.26. Humanity in all its variety exists in the very image of the divine. This affirmation of the dignity and integrity of humanity is grasped by women theologians as the basis of the prophetic demand that we 'be holy', women and men together, all races, all ethnic groups, all nationalities. Each human is to reflect the divine and be related to God the source of human being. This common assertion that all humans are created in the image of God, however, is not allowed to govern human relations. Women are therefore calling attention to this and suggesting how we may define humanity and humanness with this affirmation as our guide and then attempt to live by our definition.

Our Body—Our Difference

An element that is missing from traditional Christian anthropology is a positive appropriation of our embodiment. The necessity of facing the issue of human sexuality as an integral part of our humanness and a gift from God is a specific contribution of women theologians to religious anthropology. The fear of our bodies has made it difficult to accept the integrity of our being and led to the separation of our make up into material and spiritual, body and soul/spirit/mind. On the other hand, being in the body has allowed traditional Christian anthropology to make the female body an obstacle to the fullness of the woman's humanness (Oduyoye 1986: 130-31). On this, the women's stance is that our bodies are the medium through which we express our human-ness, as such there can be no separation of the body from the rest of our being. In consequence, women posit that the female and male bodies are not complementary, as each is capable of expressing the fullness of humanness.

Bible studies on the creation of humanity are often re-readings of Gen. 1.26 and 3.1-8, which dispute the sexual interpretation of the bib-lical stories and have sought out other biblical evidence for restoring the dignity of women. The dignity of womanhood has become a key dis-cussion in the anthropology of women. Studies, such as those done by Teresa Okure, approach this project by highlighting the participation of women in the Christian story of salvation (Okure 1992). The male and the female stand in relationship to each other as principles needing and responding to the fullness of the other. Women and men are adjudged accountable and distinct persons. They are rewarded and punished according to what they do with their humanity. The one cannot be subsumed under the other. Sexuality and spirituality as integral to our humanity is described by Betty Govinden (1996a). It is with our total humanity and as women and men that we act in history and relate one to the other.

Secondly, women's anthropology points out that what is described as feminine and masculine are culture-coded and should not be allowed to circumscribe our humanness. It is, therefore, unacceptable that women's humanness should be limited to their biology and that the cultures that make women into beings whose only reason for existence is to assure the continuity of the human race need to be transformed. Our human-ness is also expressed in our being spiritual, having a consciousness of who we are, where we come from and notions of beginnings and endings, a self-consciousness that makes us think of the meaning of life. This aspect of our being leads to notions of immortality—either its loss, or how to gain it through the perpetuation of our species. In African Religion, the divine injunction 'to increase and multiply' is not that humans may fill the earth, but so as to ensure the immortality of the human community and in some beliefs even that of the individual. Full-ness of life and immortality are won through procreation, hence the rituals and taboos associated with the human life-cycle are all geared towards preserving and enhancing life and warding off evil. For the African, that the individual is 'infinitely worthy' is asserted in the con-text of the community. It is to ensure this sense of immortality that culture has created the feminine and the masculine and ascribed gender-specific roles. The anthropology that women seek would de-emphasize our search for immortality through procreation and locate it in our diligence in living up to who we are as being in the image of God, for 'as God lives so we shall live'.[3]

The Individual is Worthy

The communal ideology that guides the humanity of Africans relativizes the worth of the individual and together with Christian 'theology of man' that of a woman in particular. Under circumstances where the individual's survival depends on staying in the group, the tendency to comply becomes the norm. In African anthropology, as in biblical anthropology, the humanity of the woman is circumscribed by her femaleness, which is rooted in notions that the woman is a wife and a mother. This is an inescapable continuum in many cultures.

Women theologians have identified marriage as a challenge to, rather than a fulfillment of, the personhood of a woman, more so than a man's. Biblical understandings, especially those located in Genesis as elaborated in Pauline writings, have served to highlight the subordination of women to men, not just of wives to husbands. And this has been accepted as the norm, in spite of Pauline teachings that should have directed attention to the worthiness of all before God and so to mutuality in man–woman relations. Whereas traditional Christian theology followed certain early Christians and Aristotelians to berate the humanness of the woman, modern theologians are more subtle, using the theme of complementarity to the same effect. There is, therefore, a perpetual challenge to women theologians in Africa to reflect on the cry of Emecheta, a prayer that people will come to realize that God has not created women to be the spare ribs of men, but to be representatives of the full humanity, unveiled by Jesus of Nazareth.

3.   The religio-culture of Africa puts emphasis on the fullness of life and immortality through procreation. This has meant that in the creative writings of West African women, marriage and child-rearing take the lion's share. In Ama Ata Aidoo's *Anowa* (1970), a wealthy couple ended their lives because they could not bear children. In Emecheta's *The Joys of Motherhood* (1979), Nnu Ego attempted suicide when her son, conceived after a long wait, died.

The shifting of this paradigm derives from women's re-reading of both the Bible and African religio-culture. Christian women find it unacceptable that we continue to live as if Christ never died or that culture is destiny. Women's anthropology insists that the prayer of Emecheta has always been the intention of God for woman-being. Nothing that derives from nature should be the cause for attributing superiority or inferiority to any human being. Women seek to underline the fact that we, women and men, are human together. They focus on the humanness of woman-being to correct the invisibility created by the notion that in the English language 'man includes woman', or worse, the application of the legal principle that the greater includes the lesser which assumes that being a woman is a being lesser than a man.

Women are seeking to pursue an anthropology that makes women and men co-responsible for the well-being of the whole community especially the family. They point out the negative influences of sayings such as 'a woman is like a banana tree that multiplies itself; a man is like a corn stalk that stands alone', for none stands alone. And the man ought to recognize his co-responsibility genetically, and in the upbringing of the children he participates in making.

If we are genuine in our affirmation of Gen. 1.26, then the worthiness of women should be a challenge to Christian anthropology. Further, women's suffering, sacrifice and spirituality, resisting evil and death should remind us of the nature of God and not of the sin and inferiority that has become associated with the humanity of woman. Anthropology should aim at our being human together. That human beings fall short of the intention of God for us is affirmed by women. That we need to re-align ourselves to God is granted by women. And that we all depend on the grace of God is admitted. Women may identify sinfulness in different acts and attitudes and some may understand 'grace' differently from the traditional dogma because of the varieties of contexts and experiences out of which we theologize. What women emphasize is that we have to live up to God's intentions, beginning with cleaning from our language all that disparages the being whom God created in God's own image.

End of Dualism

The dualism of the spiritual and the material, in traditional anthropology, assigned the material to what is worldly, and the spiritual to what pertains to our post-mortem salvation. The holistic anthropology that African women are working on dispenses with this scheme. Just as before God the male–female duality is of no account, so also the spiritual–material scheme is dispensed with by women. Human spirituality is not apart from the body and most emphatically not apart from women's bodies (Govinden 1996a). The struggle to live fully is part of the unveiling of the image of God in us. Women's anthropology incorporates all human undertakings that enhance our humanity, for they reveal who we really are meant to be. African women's spirituality should therefore be seen as a way of uncovering and advocating our humanity.

The emphasis on justice, caring, sharing and compassion even in a hostile world is the expression of the divine image all human beings are expected to reflect. It is to demonstrate humanity's given ability to respond to God and therefore tend the world around us as God would and does. This leads to the themes of reciprocity and hospitality through which African women discuss what it means to be truly human. Reciprocity is in the golden rule, as it is in Akan wisdom, and women expect men to reciprocate their respect for the humanity of the male. The human being who repays good with evil ceases to be accounted human, but the one who, in spite of evil received, returns good, is seen as exhibiting godliness which is our true humanity. It is in the same vein that women reason that if God has been so hospitable in providing for us in the world around us, we too should reciprocate by providing hospitality to others, who like us are the children of God. They look at human hospitality as a response to God's hospitality, a way of reflecting God's hospitality through our dealings with nature and in the human community.

The traditional 'doctrine of man' places human beings at the center of creation not to tend but to rule. This anthropology has worked out dualistic structures to underpin our behavior—spirit versus nature, economy parallels ecology and both lead humans to exploit nature. The human nature that women seek to heighten in their anthropology does not operate these schemes that breed oppression and exclusiveness. Women have become sensitive to this as society treats women as they treat nature by robbing them of their self-esteem, self-respect and their very humanity.

In their theology, African women have placed much emphasis on the subject of hospitality since they see it as a mark of divinity and, therefore, something to which human beings should aspire. In their writings, women affirm hospitality, but they tell of experiences of hospitality that make them feel less than human. Women, who are treated as merchandise, gifts and means of cementing relationships between men, feel less than human. The equality of the humanity of the woman and the man can only be a reality if men are made to understand that they cannot continue to be hospitable with other person's bodies and energies and skills. We do need the prophet Nathan to tell men the parable he told David.

Women would agree that to be caring and helpful, to share with, provide for and to minister to the needs of others is to be truly human. But to be made to do it, to be taken for granted when you do it, is to be treated as less than human. Choice is of the essence of humanness. The lack of respect for women's feelings and perspectives should be seen by theologians as a lack of recognition for women's humanity. The expected servanthood, servility and self-abasement are demeaning to woman's humanity. The anthropology women seek to offer would underline the fact that disrespect to woman's humanity is disrespect to total humanity and indeed disrespect to the God who made us woman and man. The dignity and worth of women is integral to the dignity and worth of humanity. There is not one humanity of the male and another of the female.

True humanity requires that we respond to God's hospitality by stewarding nature including our humanity. Women's anthropology insists that we avoid dehumanization. Women have come to the realization that they have to learn to be hospitable to themselves, to refuse the invasion of their body, a gift from God, the temple of God and the inescapable part of our humanity. The dualism of the spiritual and the material in traditional anthropology also assigned the material to what is 'this worldly' and the spiritual to what pertains to our post-mortem salvation. Women have found this inadequate, and are working on a holistic and integrated anthropology that dispenses with this dualism. They argue that human spirituality is not understood apart from the body and, most emphatically, not separate from women's bodies, because the struggle to live fully here and now is part of the unveiling of the image of God in us. Women's anthropology incorporates all human undertakings that enhance our humanity, for these efforts reveal who we really are meant to be. African women's spirituality should therefore be seen as a way of uncovering and advocating our true humanity.

Women, who suffer and experience degradation, put up a resistance because they see in those conditions a state of dehumanization. Human suffering, as such, has become part of what it means to be human, but how one discerns the root of the suffering, understands and handles suffering is what reveals the dignity of one's humanity. In women's spirituality we find that:

> Suffering grows a spirituality of persistence
> aided by faith in God who enables them to make
> a way where there is no way...
> suffering sprouts a spirituality of resistance,
> Refusing to be blamed for the hurts one endures;
> Refusing to be shamed by the violence on one's self;
> Telling when the telling itself is taboo,
> Speaking it out is half the resistance, for,
> It reveals that one is alive to one's full humanity.[4]

Resisting Dehumanization

Nyambura Njoroge, writing on 'Spirituality of Resistance and Transformation' explains that she does her reflections as an African Christian woman in search of a metaphor that will lead these women to engage in restoring their human dignity and respect for life (Njoroge 1996). Like Emecheta, Njoroge seeks to underline the humanity of women as they exhibit courage, determination and inner strength to confront callousness, violence and death and to transform them into caring and decency. Women who, with dignity, challenge and oppose oppressive powers in biblical and African history, are the models of humanity that women theologians promote. Adu-Ampoma (1996) refers to Yaa Asantewa, a 'Queen-Mother' Edweso in Ghana who challenged British colonial arrogance, as follows: 'Yaa Asantewa stands for the best in humanity, the disgust for oppression, a demonstration of courage and determination'.

Women resist dehumanization when they refuse to develop 'feelings of inadequacy or humiliation that attack their innermost integrity of the self' (Ackermann 1996b: 146). Women believe in the dignity of all human beings and would not stand having their humanity degraded, for that is tantamount to being robbed of it. The words of Flora, a South

---

4.   Author's own construction. However, the third line is a direct quotation from Williams 1993: 198.

African women have made their own the Womanist theologian Dolores Williams' insightful study of Hagar in her book, *Sisters in the Wilderness*.

African woman's reflection on the aims of 'Ritual School' sums up this resistance to dehumanization:

> This unconditional obedience to the will of men and their whims was something against which women instinctively rebelled, despite having been to ritual school. But that rebellion had an enormous cost... Yet I was prepared to bear the cost, if the price I paid resulted in my becoming the strong and independent woman I knew I could be, and longed to become. I yearned to be a liberated woman who needed a man for the right reasons—reasons of friendship, mutual respect and support, trust, reciprocal dependence, and love, which, in going beyond mere sex and child bearing, encompassed the feelings and the soul. I knew I had the potential to become such a woman, despite what I had been through and the world in which I lived (Mathabane 1994: 213).

Women's struggle for survival in Africa is not only a struggle to stay alive. It seeks a quality of life that can be truly and fully human not only for themselves but also for men. When women refuse to stay on the margins, they are making a statement concerning their understanding of what it means to be human. The spirituality of resistance therefore enables one to hold on to one's humanity. Resisting anonymity is an expression of the belief that our individual humanity is meant to find expression in community.

Responsibility and Reciprocity

The emphasis on justice, caring, sharing and compassion, even in a hostile world, is the expression of the divine image all human beings are expected to reflect. It is to demonstrate the human given ability to respond to God, and therefore to tend to the world around us as God would and does. This leads us to the themes of responsibility, reciprocity and hospitality through which African women discuss what it means to be truly human. If being human is reflecting the divine, then we do need to look at God's hospitality and how we reflect this in our dealings with nature and in the human community.

Human beings have tended to place themselves in the center of creation. Traditional Christian anthropology has fostered this and worked out dualistic structures to underpin our behavior—spirit versus nature, economy paralleled ecology—and both lead humans to exploit nature. The human nature that woman seek to heighten in their anthropology does not operate these schemes that breed oppression and exclusiveness.

Society treats women as they treat nature, robbing them of their self-esteem, self-respect and their very humanity.

In the theology of African women some effort has been made to reconceptualize hospitality. It is a mark of divinity and is expected of all humanity but African women have experiences of hospitality that makes them feel less than human. The lack of respect for women's feelings and perspectives is seen by theologians as a lack of recognition of women's humanity. The expected servanthood, servility and self-abasement are demeaning to women's humanity. The anthropology women seek to offer would underline the fact that disrespect to women's humanity is disrespect to humanity and the God who made us woman and man. It is as if one were to say God made a mistake making me woman. On the other hand, true humanity requires that we respond to God's hospitality by tending nature and honoring our humanity.

The Chewa myth referred to above ends with God counseling that human beings live in harmony and apologize when we have wronged, and honor God in whose image we are made. In the myth it is man's envy of the procreative power of women that is the source of disharmony. In our world we need an anthropology that will enable us to benefit from the diversity of gender, race, language and nationality. Women theologians are seeking to contribute to the reconceptualizing of such an anthropology—one that will take seriously the principles of participation and inclusiveness.

Chapter Six

The Household of God: Studies in Ecclesiology

In Africa, home-making is a major part of women's experience so it provides a point of theological reflection on all that has to do with community, unity, ecumenism, participation and, above all, the relationship between creation and God. When Alice Lenshina established The Church of the New Jerusalem in open protest against Roman Catholic missionaries in Zambia, she introduced several traditional household religious concepts and practices that the patriarchal Bena Ngandu and later Christianity had abolished. Most specifically she built her church on 'the bored stone' principle which kept married couples faithful to each other and in which women were the mediators between the family and the divine. On Christology she taught that Jesus was the suffering servant who takes on the pain of women. Jesus is partner and helper. The imagery of this church is intensely family based. Women expect the Church to be a household in which all can feel at home because all are accounted worthy.

However, in an article, a sociologist, Felicia I. Ekejiuba, disputes the use of 'household' to describe the setting of the African family, and proposes instead the word 'hearth-holds'. She argues that the householder is not necessarily the focal point of the well-being of that community. Africans, she says, are organized around the hearths of women, some of whom may be biological mothers but not necessarily so (Ekejiuba 1995).[1] This agrees with the images of God as Mother in some traditions, and as provider and sustainer in Christianity. It agrees also with images of the compassionate Jesus, who cared so much for the physical

---

1. Hearth-hold is defined as all who are nourished from the same fore-place. This Nigerian sociologist defines hearth-hold as 'a woman and all her dependants whose food security she is either fully or partially responsible for'.

and mental well-being of all he encountered. It also fits the Holy Spirit, the advocate and comforter many of whose attributes reflect the mothering on which African society depends. When in African Religion we speak of the children of God, we mean all human beings. All human beings are the people of God. They belong to God's household housed on this planet and around God in the unseen realms. All of creation is cared for by God, the source of our being. The whole cosmos constitutes the *oikonomia* of God. In God's household religious people discern many hearth-holds. It has, therefore, become important for women theologians that they see the Church as the hearth-hold of Christ within the household of God. In Africa we cannot operate on the basis of a triumphant Christology that claims that all are Christians whether they know it or not. We can only hope that the 'household of God' will, one day, become the hearth-hold of Christ, who is not the monopoly of Christians.

The Bible, too, is no stranger to women-headed households—Hagar and Ishmael; Martha, Mary and Lazarus; Lydia and her household. It is, therefore, meaningful for women to see the African household as providing Africans with a model of community through which to discern the characteristics of a community under God (Oduyoye 1995: 238-54).

The picture of the Jerusalem community of Christians painted by Luke in Acts is a model of the hearth-hold of Jesus. The courage of the people who dared to witness to their faith that Jesus of Nazareth was the anointed one of God had stayed together for mutual support and encouragement. They were living in a hostile world, a world of unbelief. They were not only a minority in numbers but they were also beginning to transform the meaning of the traditional family and house-hold by bringing together women and men, related only through their faith in Jesus Christ. They had become a hearth-hold on the model of the Nigerian woman sociologist. They have become a community that resembles an extension of mother–child relations, a community whose 'food security', whose faith in God, is nourished by Jesus.

For the Christian community the witness of Jesus of Nazareth to the reign of God, has resulted in images of a world ruled, managed or directed by God. African women use the traditional terminologies of 'kingdom' and 'reign', but they also find meaningful the term *kindom* as kinship is central to human relations in Africa and Christologies, and this phrase is common in sermons and in theological writings. The Circle has employed 'commonwealth' in some of its deliberations. They have also joined others in promoting the biblical imagery of the 'household' to designate the human community under God. The church is indeed a hearth-hold with God as mother, the whole earth is the hearth and all human beings as the children of God. Dealing with the Church, however, they would specifically see a community that claims special relationship with Jesus of Nazareth who was named the Christ.

Women and the Church

> I am not giving up! To church I must go
> First worship day I walk in with great hope
> But from the pulpit I hear from the preacher
> 'Thus says the Bible
> "Wives submit to your husbands in all things"
> No woman is allowed to speak in church
> Their husbands have all the answers to their questions'
> (Agumba 1997: 154-55).

Agumba's poem, 'The Search for my Place' utilizes the first five of the seven stanzas encouraging and strengthening the African woman with the kiSwahili word 'Tulia', *Keep Calm*. These stanzas are a lament over being treated as ancillary to the family, which really belongs only to the men. In the sixth stanza, when woman decides to seek a place where she could truly belong, she goes to church. Here she had to ask, who or what is the church? Do I really belong here?

I shall use 'Church' in a general way to cover the organized expression of Christianity in Africa. The nuancing of the Church, church and churches has its validity. But the ecclesiology of African women is not focused on that line of investigation. It moves from images of the Church in the New Testament, to the churches of the African women's experience.[2] The way women narrate their experiences of the Church can be an indication of what they understand the Church to be.[3] There

2.   This is a subject on which much feminist theological literature abounds. The aim here is to pursue the discussion with the assumption that the theological and ecclesiological arguments from Scripture and tradition are familiar. Much of this is rehearsed by African women, but in addition they employ a cultural hermeneutic to re-read the Bible stories with a view to clarifying for themselves the dogma that rules women's experience of the church.

3.   The Ecumenical Decade, Churches in Solidarity with Women (The Decade) which was launched by member churches of the World Council of Churches (WCC) in 1988 has provided resources for gathering together women's relationship to the

is much focus on the churches' attitudes to and teaching about women, which indicates what the Church is, as opposed to what it claims to be. This ecclesiology does not dwell on the catholicity or universality of the Church beyond the fact that when it comes to the experience of women, the Church is truly universal. Studies undertaken at various periods by the WCC show that there is a great deal of similarity in the way women, worldwide, experience the Church. Nowhere do we find churches in which the unity of the Church is seriously pursued when it comes to the unity of humanity, and certainly not the unity as regards the genders, for nowhere are women and men treated as being on an equal footing in the Church.

As far as attitudes are concerned, this way of viewing women in the Church is found not only among men but among women too. Often one finds that African women have so internalized this low esteem of women in the Church and other prevailing values that they become accomplices in the suppression of their own gender. This is most obvious in the question of ordination, but that is not the only instance in which the Church is divided against itself. Women see the Church as divided against itself for as long as it militates against and marginalizes women. In general, women's experience of the Church is no different from the culture outside the Church structures. Often they experience more recognition of their humanity outside of the Church, while their suppression in socioculture is referred back to religious teachings and demands, in this case of the Church. Alina Machema from Lesotho writes:

> Although Christianity has long been experienced in Africa and has preached that Jesus Christ came to liberate everybody irrespective of sex, race, strength or financial status, African women have been locked up in a safe compartment together with their good ideas (Machema 1990: 131).

church and their words about the church. The predecessor study 'Community of Women and Men in Church and Society' stimulated a lot of interest and has resulted in further studies. The Decade is producing more. Harare (1998) saw the end of 'The Decade' but it remains part of our theological journey and, hopefully, will spin off further mileage. My book, *Who Will Roll the Stone Away?* (Oduyoye 1988: 69) sets out an African Resurrection hope that inspires women's theology, while the Jesus birth story at the end of the book is our inspiration that goes counter-culture when we deem that to be the mind of God.

What, then, is the Church to Women?

The language of women about the Church often indicates that the Church dismisses the pain of women or treats it lightly. Often the language of the Church puts women down. Women speak of the Church's neuroses and double standards with regard to human sexuality. Hypocrisy reigns in the Church when it is men who need to change their ways. Often women's power is denied and their experiences rejected. Very often women work in the Church and men take credit for the outcome. The sin, sex and women triad has warped the community of women and men in the Church.

The Church prides itself on being in the world, but not of the world. Where it lags behind society in its recognition of women, its leaders claim that the justice and equality demanded by women is of the world's agenda and does not bind the Church into re-examining its teaching about and treatment of women. Musimbi Kanyoro describes the churches as 'encultured', that is, they take on the cultures of the communities that generated them. But, observing the struggles of women, the situation has to be described in diverse ways. Some churches refuse to be 'of the world' in the sense that where 'the world' would grant women access on the basis of human rights and justice, some churches would still refuse because of particular doctrines and histories. Again Kanyoro states that the status of women within the Church is a microcosm of their status within society of which the Church is a part. For, even when the rights of women are enshrined in laws, custom, tradition, popular attitudes and values lag far behind and continue to oppress women. She says that, regrettably, the Church is more often than not a part of this oppressive culture. Even when the Church has the institutions and mechanisms for the participation of women, it has few of the practices.

Women's Solidarity with the Church

The Church's silences over women's subordination, over the violence and discrimination against women, the hypocrisy around sexuality and men's lack of solidarity, all mark the Church of women's experience as different from the Church that can be the body of Christ and the hearth-hold of Jesus. Not infrequently, therefore, the question is asked, 'Why are women filling the churches, given the Church's lack of solidarity with women?' Others ask, 'Are women not part of the Church? Why do women exclude themselves from what the Church has become?' These questions apply to different aspects of the Church's life. As far as attitudes towards women are concerned, many church women in Africa are no different from men.

We have to take into consideration the fact that it is the Church's teaching arising out of men's interpretations of the Bible and the Church's history that the women have come to disparage themselves. As Joyce Tsabedze points out, the Bible is not univocal on women's participation in the Church. Allowing a men-only perspective to rule the Church has given the Church an understanding of itself that is not holistic (Tsabedze 1990). We also cannot overlook the fact that women are not in a position to affect the decisions that the churches take concerning women or any other matters. The constant plea for integration and insistence on co-responsibility is evidence of how women experience the Church. Rachel Tetteh writes:

> I believe in living in a house of order peace and concord but I also believe that all people including women have the right to participate fully in the activities of the church. Racism, tribalism, classism and sexism are problems that have confronted the church over the years (Tetteh 1990b: 157).

Women's solidarity, therefore, is with the Church as they see it through the eyes of Jesus. Women's solidarity is with the Church that they envision Christ represents. They know the real Church and its shortcomings as well as its strengths. They remain in the Church because they are called by the Christ to do so.

In Africa even as participation and justice—including the ordination of women—continue to be disputed, women remain in solidarity with the Church. They are convinced that the call and the task of the Church are to identify the existing suffering and name it. They will not give up the belief that the Church is confronted with injustices and deals with them in the name of God. They are in the Church because it is expected to bring joy and abundant life. Their hope is that God will liberate the Church from gender dualism and make all real participants in this household of God.

There are only a few who will say they stay in the Church because they hope to participate in transforming the Church from within. More realistic is the view that they stay in to nurture one another. The Church provides one more umbrella organization, like the traditional markets of West Africa, for women to get together and 'do their own thing'. Building their women's organizations within the Church provides security and solace. Women experience the caring solidarity of Jesus and not the oppression of the structures operated mainly by men. They know that if the Church were truly following the example of Jesus, then women would be sent out with the Good News; so they find their own methods of doing just that (see James 1990: 173). Women create for themselves a church within the Church, 'a church in the round' that they seek within the pyramidal Church run by the men. Without seeking directly to influence the men, we have seen in Africa the rise of men's groups in African churches. Will this bring about an awareness of mutual accountability before God concerning the being and the doing of the Church, or is it a simple acknowledgment that as far as gender is concerned the unity of the church is in jeopardy?

Sharing and Participation

The language of the Church often suggests that women are not integral to its being. What does a woman do when she is requested to respond to the question 'and women. Where do they come in?' when a church is reviewing its understanding of ministry?[4] This is an issue on which many African women theologians have reflected (cf. Eneme 1986: 29). Grace Eneme calls for the integration of women into the Church as living stones. In a sermon on 2 Peter, Eneme posits that the oppression of women in Christ's Church is antithetical to the image of the Church as an edifice. It makes women into stones that have been rejected by those who have named themselves the builders of the Church. Staying with this metaphor one could say that, at best, women are decorative stones and therefore dispensable. It means, as Bette Ekeya observes, that 'for the majority of women the Good News which is the person of Jesus Christ is still inaccessible... Unless church structures radically change to allow women to receive the liberty which the Son of God died to make

---

4.   In response, the text read at the Conference of Methodist Church Nigeria (MCN), 1976 at Ibadan had the title 'Order in the Community of Women and Men in the Church'. MCN publishing house preferred the original question put to me, adding as subtitle 'Women in the Church'. Are we church? Are we or are we not an integral part of the human race? This is my question and that of the theologians of The Circle.

available, there can be no real transformation of people's lives' (Ekeya 1986: 59). Sharing fully in the life of the Church, its mission and ministry is the calling of all who are in the church. Thus, the Church of women's experience, has yet to be recognized.

Justice, participation, inclusiveness and ministry are the most frequent concepts that generate discussion of the Church's self-understanding among African women. For the 1996 conference of The Circle, the discussion of ecclesiology was organized around the concept of *koinonia*. Women wrote on inequalities and lack of democracy in the Church, which results in women being treated as junior partners rather than as daughters in God's house. The Church ought to be a *koinonia*, the sharing of a common life, said Molee Boame of Zaire.[5] Sharing a common life means working together, using the best one can give and not according to the limitations that tradition and culture associates with one's gender. Others, like Nkebi Lwamba (Zaire) focused on justice, pointing out that injustice destroys *koinonia* understood as a community of believers who constitute a communion. And, from the Zairian situation, Vibila Vuadi illustrates the injustices of African culture and the church's history.

Amarech Getachew (Ethiopia) sees women's lack of decision making in the Church as injustice because it constitutes a denial of equal rights in Church and society. Equity, equality and equal rights are concepts that many church people dispute, but which women theologians are putting forward as issues the Church ought to re-examine in the context of the theology of creation and in view of the anthropology that women are proposing. They point out the injustice of treating women as property, thus preventing them from exercising free will as befits human beings. 'Community', they posit, is destroyed where there is inequality and 'power over' others. For women mutuality is a cardinal mark of *koinonia*.

Using New Testament models, the women describe a Church that is true to its origins as one in which women and men participate in evangelization on the basis of God-given graces. The denial of ordination to women is, therefore, seen as a deliberate ploy to keep women one step behind men in the service that all are called to render in God's household. By so doing, the Church has succeeded in turning ordination into a mark of power conferring rights reserved to men. Those who ordain

---

5.   Zaire has become Democratic Republic of the Congo.

women imbue the women with the same attitudes, so that ordained women behave towards other women as having been endued with *extra* authority and *extra* holiness. For the Church to be a true *koinonia* this attitude towards ordination has got to change and the model of priest-hood of all believers honored in actuality. It also calls for a re-imagin-ing of the mission of the Church and the ministries required for its accomplishment.

Partnership of women and men, ordained or not, is the true image of the Church of Christ. To all the members of the hearth-hold of Jesus have been given charisms for the building up of the community, says Edith Semmambo of Uganda. African women's concern for participa-tion centers on the injustices involved in the limits and burdens that women experience in the Church and in society. If *koinonia* is a com-munity of sharing and participation, then, in its operations, women too should find power to exercise their charisms for the general health of the community and especially for the Church. The experiences of African women suggest that the Church in Africa is not ready to do anything towards becoming a true *koinonia*. Rakotosaholy from Madagascar points at the brokenness of Church and society caused by violence against women and the neglect of their participation. Many African women theologians, like Josephine Gitome, put their hope in education as the instrument of justice and participation, so that the Church might become the household of God, a true *koinonia*.

Justice as part of the foundation of *koinonia* is the theme explored in *Daughters of Anowa* (Oduyoye 1995: chs. 7–8). Justice is viewed from the point of right-action judged by the compassion of God in response to the situations of oppression and vulnerability. The emphasis is on equity and mutuality. In a true communion no voices are left unheard and no God-given charisms are trivialized or glossed over. Here Oduyoye calls the Church to be a real model of a community in which all have the possibility to participate. The community has to live out its proclaimed *raison d'être* based on the life of the Christ who came that all may have abundant life. Abundant life, it is argued, is that which is nurtured in a communion where there is participation. Participation, we should note, is different from gender-directed, predetermined forms of involvement that African cultures operate. It has no room for subordination. The Church should be a place of mutual caring, sharing of skills and other resources. She points to biblical passages that will help the Church to grow into the *koinonia* Christ intends it to be (for example, Prov. 22.17-

18 and Eph. 5.28-31). The Church should show itself to be a community of caring if it is to represent the body of Christ.

Caring and Mission

In the women's theology, ecclesiology goes together with missiology. The reason for the Church's being is to be at work in God's mission. The Church is expected to lift people up from the sighs and the groanings, and put their feet on the route to the promised peace of God. Denise Ackermann, writing on a quest for healing, stated that 'participation and inclusiveness for those living for the reign of God are based in Christ's injunction "you must love your neighbor as yourself".' In the Church's mission, there cannot be any 'isms' to divide the human race. She goes on to elaborate that 'inclusiveness lies at the heart of the Great Commandment, and that participation is the active response to the assent to inclusiveness'. The Church and all who are associated with it are called to take part in 'healing actions' (Ackermann 1996a: 145-46). This ministry of healing and caring is the African women's emphasis on the *raison d'être* of the Church.

Women argue the call for inclusiveness also on the basis of our common baptism. Baptism, women say, is the rite that confers 'citizenship' in God's Commonwealth, writes Jessica Nakawombe in Kanyoro and Njoroge (1996: 40). In the community of the Church, women should take part in defining and cultivating the ethos in which all will thrive as God wills us to do. Women must be included in the identification of what is good news, for what harms women cannot be good news for the whole community. What brings death to women cannot be said to bring life to the community. The Church therefore misses out on its vocation when it refuses to listen to and include women in its task of being in God's mission. No health, healing or empowerment in and by the Church is complete when women are excluded.

Given the context of the theology, we find mission being described as a mediation of salvation, often in terms of liberation, humanization and the pursuit of justice for all, but especially for those totally deprived of it, namely women. The mission is the task of the whole Church to the whole human community. However women insist that it should have a special focus on and by women for whom patriarchy in Christianity has been bad news. To evangelize a people using notions and structures of patriarchy does not become the Church of Christ. The Church's participation in God's mission entails working for and with goodness;

that is justice, love, peace and wholeness. It should bring about the flourishing of righteousness that will bring joy through the appreciation and appropriation of the gift of diversity. The Church should be in mission to bring about 'critical non-hierarchical involvement with the other'. This would be a demonstration of the caring that Jesus expects from the Church that continues his earthly life.

Redeeming the Church

Women's experience of the Church and their words on the Church have been further highlighted through reports of visits to churches in Africa confirming what women of The Circle have said and written. Redeeming the Church begins with breaking the silence around the Church's attitudes to, and teachings concerning women. Redeeming the Church involves encouraging action against the divisiveness of sexism, racism, tribalism and exploitation. The image of the Church as a caring community is tarnished by its tardiness in confronting violence against women, worse, in participating in the marginalization and demeaning of women. The unity of the Church can only become a reality if the Church works intentionally on the call to be an inclusive community. Women uphold the unity of the Church in their songs:

> I am the Church
> You are the Church
> We are together the Church
> All who follow Jesus,
> All who follow Jesus round the world;
> Yes, we are the Church together.

If we are the Church together, then together we must we must fulfill the *raison d'etre* of the Church. 'Together' means together as women and men, together as north and south, together as black and white (Oduyoye and Kanyoro 1990: 34). The Church must become a household in which all count, and in which the full range of ministries become the joint responsibility of all in the Church and are undertaken according to charisms. Agumba in her poem asserts, 'Nobody can send me out of the church, for I have a message for the disciples' (Agumba 1997: 155). Women ground their worthiness to participate in God's mission through the church on the call to Mary of Magdala, to 'Go...tell!'

Finally, the Church cannot describe itself as holy and mean that it is separate from the world and the world's agenda. Stating doctrines inside the Church will not liberate unless the Church gets out into the streets, heals the sick and confronts the unjust. The Church is in the world that God loved, and has to work for the well-being of the world. Seeing that God's presence cannot be limited to organized Christianity, the Church does well to see where God is at work and to promote those salvific acts. Wherever the image of God in humans is promoted, the Church should be present to enhance that effort. Based on a historical study of the Moravian Church of South Africa, Angelene Swart writes: 'The church has to continue the servanthood of Jesus Christ on earth. She sees the participation of women in the total picture of this servanthood.' She states further: 'I do believe that women have been called together with men to actualize the servanthood role of the church in the world' (Swart 1990: 148). Having a male-dominated hierarchy in the Church clouds this servanthood, for the ministry as operated by men seeks to be served rather than to serve.

The ecclesiological emphasis that women bring, is that which holds the Church accountable to being a community that lives the life of Christ, that preaches the reign and love of God by its being and doing, serves God's people and God's purposes and presents itself as a sample of *koinonia* approved of and by God, and in which God participates.

Chapter Seven

Hospitality and Spirituality

A pregnant young woman from the rural area came to her brother in the city to get ready to have her baby. For weeks after the baby had arrived, the young mother could not decide whether to return to her village, for life was more agreeable in the city. So what was to be done? The situation became embarrassing for Evènasse and her husband. Even more awkward for the couple was that Evènasse's mother-in-law approved of this prolonged and unreasonable stay. This was becoming a dangerously parasitic situation because her sister-in-law had become a menace for her nephews against whom she grumbled at the least opportunity.[1]

This is a commonplace occurrence in Africa's extended family system, which often becomes conflictual. The system worked in the rural areas and in the pastoral and agricultural communities where all contributed to the household economy. But in towns, increasingly, those who arrive only do so to sponge on the salary earners and the traders. Not because they do not want to work, but because there is often nothing for them to do. After an analysis of her story Marguerite continues: 'In spite of this we Christian women have to fight for the abiding good of hospitality, because this African practice corresponds with our Christian duty as in Luke 10:40. "The one who receives you receives me, the one who receives me, receives the one who sent me." ' Therefore, as Christians, we have no choice but to obey Jesus even in the context of the changing culture. It is necessary to preserve the values and the richness of our culture that are also Christlike.

---

1. A real life story presented by Marguerite Couthin Fassinou (Kahungu and Fassinou 1996: 18-20). Evènasse is the wife in the host family in the city.

The women's literature on this subject also includes several traditional folktales, myths and legends as well as readings from the writings on African Religion (Oduyoye and Kanyoro 1990: 9-54; Oduyoye 1995: 19-55). These reveal the principles around which women's lives revolve:

> Take care you do not rise too far above your peers or else you will be called a witch; one does not destroy the one whom one mothers, and many others.

To this women theologians respond: 'It is one thing to be a subject of voluntary self-sacrifice and entirely another to be the object whose self-sacrifice is involuntary or who is as unwilling victim.' These are the notions that this chapter sets out to examine. The chapter is also rooted in the theological reflections on baptism. The argument will be that our baptism into Christ compels us to see a new humanity, free and tuned into mutual sharing of gifts and a sustaining community (Oduyoye 1986: 138-45).

Gertrude Tundu Kialu from Zaire, referring to Genesis 18, Romans 12 and 13 and several other biblical passages, points out that African hospitality is very close to that of the world of the Bible and especially of the Gospel (Kialu 1996: ch. 10). Kialu says 'Women are so close to God', suggesting that as God's rain falls on all regardless, so women's hospitality should be abundant, free and all inclusive. Going even further is Ebenye Mbondo's claim that 'What women want is what God wants'[2] (Mbondo 1996: 11). She asserts that without women's tenderness and hospitality, security at home would be impossible, for as she claims, 'The other sex is not so committed to such things'. Mbondo glorifies women's role in the home as those who make 'life more poetic', but admits that paradoxically, they are also the ones who are the object of violence and intimidation. So she does introduce the element of the exploitation of hospitality.

In her analysis she sees that all this is changing and the hospitality of yesterday is disappearing. People are no longer preoccupied with the safety of the stranger who knocks on the door. No longer are people keen to reserve the best drinking vessels for strangers. Hospitality can no longer be guaranteed to create friendships. All has changed, other cultures, other styles of life, modernity, the technology we acquire with brutality, especially in the urban areas, have undermined the goodwill that was the origin of hospitality. They are incompatible with traditional

---

2. My translation of 'ce que femme veut, Dieu le veut'.

African hospitality. And yet the residue remains, namely, the right to protection that visitors could expect. In the turmoil of Africa, refugees are received in the 'modern' camps for the masses, but the small groups that arrive meld into the local population, especially if they have the same language. Homes are still open to refugees. Some are given land to build and even decide to stay on when the crisis that drove them out is overcome. It is when the scale becomes overwhelming that camps become inevitable. So then what we are dealing with is the inevitable modification of cultural practices to respond to the exigencies of the changing times and circumstances.

The Malagasy say: 'Better to lose your money than to lose your human relations.' Marie Erison (in Kahungu and Fassinou 1996: 33) also adds that to receive a visitor is to honor the person. You receive visitors before you ask for their identities. This is what our ancestors have handed down to us. Mariamo (in Kahungu and Fassinou 1996: 34), also from Madagascar, affirms that this is a moral law and accords well with the Christian compassion that we learn from God and from Jesus Christ. Thus hospitality is given a religious meaning, and linked with the ancestors, Christ and God. It is seen as inherent in being African, as well as in adhering to a religion that derives from the Bible. Mary, they say, played host to God and became 'Theotokos', mother of God. Thus Christian women are linked in a special way to hospitality. This is the context in which Nkebi Lwamba (in Kahungu and Fassinou 1996: 35-36) of the Democratic Republic of Congo (DRC) would say that women are proud to be hospitable, and the ancestors reward hospitality with prosperity. Women are more than half of Africa's population and if they continue the traditional practice, then it has a future.

Nevertheless this ideal of women is not asserted naively. Lwamba describes how rich women pass by poor women with babies in arms without so much as throwing a glance, while poor women would often give. The forest belt of West and Central Africa from Côte d'Ivoire to DRC played host to people from the drought-stricken areas in the 1980s and again in the 1990s. During these periods the picture of Hagar and baby Ishmael returns to haunt African women again and again, and moves them to be 'the face of God', even in their own poverty. The women also observe that people in power are often heartless, and so cannot be hospitable. They enrich themselves without thought for the poor. It is obvious, therefore, that hospitality is not being presented as a panacea for Africa's ills, nor are women being portrayed as the saviors of

Africa, whose self-sacrificing hospitality is impeccable. What is being said here is that hospitality is a reality in Africa, that it has religious roots and that it is a moral debt. Hospitality is linked with economy. Hospitality can establish lasting friendships and alliances, where there is reciprocity. 'Give a handful of roasted groundnuts to a stranger and you will receive even more in the future'. We are also aware that hospitality can be perverted. We are aware that providing hospitality can be risky, but then, did God not take a risk to hand over this beautiful earth to human beings? There are multifarious aspects of hospitality that call for examination; in this chapter we limit ourselves to the relation between hospitality and parasitism, hospitality and sexuality, and gather the thoughts together under hospitality as a lifestyle. We do all this in the context of how the word is understood and practiced in Africa.

Defining Hospitality

Rose-Zoe Obianga, from a review of literature in French and her experience as a Cameroonian and a well-travelled African, asserts what we often hear, that Africans are unanimous that hospitality is a fundamental African value. This phrase is echoed in many papers, written for a conference of The Circle held in Douala, Cameroon in 1994 before Obianga delivered the keynote address for the conference. It is one phrase that endures in spite of the many qualifications, anomalies and aberrations. It is a valuable principle, is what women are saying. Obianga herself asks, 'What is hospitality in the midst of Africa's horrors?' It is from her paper that I now present the four concepts that make the meaning of hospitality, slightly expanded by myself. They are: (1) welcoming/receiving, reception; (2) charity/almsgiving; (3) boarding and lodging/hotel, hospital; and (4) protecting/sanctuary, integration. Receptions, hospices, hospitals, hotels and even integration, as in acquiring citizenship, have monetary price tags in our contemporary experience. But hospitality, as in African tradition, only hopes for reciprocity should the need arise.

Offering and receiving hospitality is a key indication of the African emphasis on sustaining our life-force at all costs, both as individuals and as communities. Life is our most valuable asset, so preserving life and prolonging life is a way of life in Africa. The paradox is that this makes us vulnerable. Hospitality is built on reciprocity, openness and acceptance, but to open one's self to the other is always a risk. To preserve life

Africans are ready to compromise and to accommodate even what erodes their dignity, weakens their present and mortgages their future. Obianga observes that offering and receiving hospitality brings both opportunity and risk. It is an opportunity for a revelation, an epiphany of the as yet unknown and thus unexperienced. What are the intentions of the guest? What are the intentions of the one who offers hospitality? (Obianga 1996). These are not theoretical questions.

Once on my way to a conference in the USA I found at the airport that there was no one to meet me. A couple on the same flight, who must have noticed my consternation, came to me. I explained my situation. They not only offered to take me to the conference center; as it happened, they hosted me in their home for the night and then took me to the center after breakfast, and all was well. When I told my story and at all subsequent tellings my hearers have looked at me incredulously: 'You are a woman of faith' is the usual response, always followed with the foolishness of the risk, told in terms of harrowing narrations of all that could have happened to me. My angels of the day also took a risk taking me home. I have childhood experiences as a Pastor's child to confirm my assertion, but none of them could stop the practice of hospitality in a Methodist Mission House.

As Justine Kahungu (1996: 56) asserts, one can arrive any time of day and night without notice or prior arrangement, and one will receive '*ce qu'il y a de meilleur*'. No bills, and upon leaving, you are directed on the best way to go and accompanied until you are actually on it. But the guest is expected to leave a blessing behind. And I did. And until today, continue to bless this couple whose name I now even forget, but God never forgets a deed of hospitality. That is my faith as an African.

The exploitation of hospitality did not stop my parents and does not stop traditional Africa, but it is still a risk. Our best stories and revelations of the human character come with the many people who passed through the Mission House and touched our lives. All these people must have reinforced our life-force. But they were also extra responsibility for us all. Openness and acceptance of the other remains a positive quality in Africa. Hospitality, says Rose-Zoe Obianga, offers opportunity for friendship and is a force for renewal. Mary and Joseph received the Christ-child and the world was never the same again. Africans welcomed Europeans and adopted European values, but the element of reciprocity was missing. Many Africans did not close themselves to the values of outsiders. As she reminds us, many resisted and continue to do so, when the outside values are deemed incompatible with African norms. All fought to varying degrees what was obvious exploitation and those who would take advantage of our hospitality. As with the instructions given in *The Didache*, Julius Nyerere of Tanzania linked hospitality with work and economic productivity: 'Treat your guests as guests for two days, and on the third day, give them hoes.' That is, put them to work doing whatever you do to sustain your hospitality. Hospitality demands that we teach not only life-skills but also specifically economic skills in order to prevent dependence and parasitism.

In contemporary Africa, this principle is applied to refugees and displaced persons, of which Africa has no lack. Before the international approach entered the scene to establish camps, the traditional African system presupposed eventual assimilation. Refugees are no longer strangers. A stranger is the one who comes in from outside; another continent, another race another civilization, another worldview. Strangers are people with other values, other perspectives, other objectives, other principles of life. Openness vis-à-vis 'the other', however you define the 'other', is offering of hospitality. Viewed theologically, Obianga points out that 'the other is indeed God,' who visits us.

The Bible has examples of these 'visitors'. 'God', says Obianga, 'visited through other persons, though at the beginning God did so *personally*.' Here she was referring to the visit paid to Eve and Adam in the garden of Eden at the beginning of time. Thereafter we have God visiting through other persons: messengers/angels, prophets, many other women and men of God, Jesus, other Christ figures. Obianga and other Africans also see God's hospitality to us in Jesus. God gives us lodgings, feeds us and, as in Gen. 18.2, expects us to lodge others. Paul, in his letters, calls for relief for Christians in Jerusalem and commends the impressive generosity of the Macedonians. But he began to earn his own living after staying a while with friends at Ephesus. The parallels and examples from the Bible are many but the basic theme of women is that God's hospitality to us, our claim to being in the image of God, points us to the practice of love as God's love is in us. Therefore, Obianga concludes that in our days African Christians do not exercise hospitality solely because it is a fundamental virtue of our African traditional society, but also and, above all, because it is derived from our faith in Jesus who for us is the way, the truth and the life.

Hospitality and Economy

Catherine Murigande, who offered the paper on the economic context of hospitality in Africa to the French-speaking conference, highlighted a fact which Nyambura in the Eastern and Southern Africa conference, states as follows: 'Women are forced to sacrifice their lives simply to feed their children' (Murigande 1996: 25). Women therefore become the poorest of the poor, and are the sacrifice that the Western economies demand if others are to be rich and successful. Murigande, reviewing Mt. 25.31-45, reads the African situation as one in which taking hospitality seriously led Africans to act in a Christ-like fashion even before Christ had been preached to them. She surmises that it is the moral values already present in African communities that greatly helped evangelization of the continent. She indicates that the hospitality taught in the Bible has affinity with the African cultural characteristics of sharing, welcoming and solidarity. The burden of her input, however, is that, today, hospitality is strained by the degradation of Africa's economies, a Third World phenomenon, the experience of which brings to mind the Akan saying: '*Ohia na ema Okanni ye aboa*.'[3] Certainly, one even has to add an apology to the animal world, for what this saying indicates is that poverty means more than lack of economic resources, it also means a loss of human dignity.

Traditionally, life in Africa was linked to land and family. We are part of nature and part of the human community, says Murigande, and each of us is expected to contribute towards assuring the continuity of family prosperity. Traditionally, families worked together towards self-sufficiency and even now the dependency syndrome flows outside the circle of family members only when all of that has proved insufficient. Daily work, family relations, religious rites, education, formation of children, all, are linked with 'forming an undifferentiated unity' Children are brought up among other things to live by the notions of sharing, solidarity and welcoming of neighbors, family, acquaintances and strangers. This was African hospitality and for some people still is. Sharing and solidarity covers all aspects of life, land, farming, food, drink, joyful events, sad events—all are experienced in community, all are in one way or another the shared experience of the whole community. Hospitality was natural.

3.   'It is poverty that turns an Akan person into an animal.'

But today, hospitality though important in our rhetoric and for our survival, is beginning to weaken as the traditional mechanisms that supported it are going. Most threatened of them is the extended family. It is gradually being replaced by the nuclear family and the social phenomenon of individualism. It seems that the modern economic development and its globalization have no room for African hospitality. The Western model of industrialization, which altered European community ethos, is eroding that of the whole world—including Africa. Capital and technology do not seem to have any respect for land and people, and Africa now imports both capital and technology besides the ideology of individualism. 'The western economic model, into which colonialism helped to suck Africa, has undermined its food security,' a basic element for human survival, says Murigande (1996: 23). This situation, she says, has arisen because profit has no use for subsistence agriculture and Africans throughout the ages have depended on this system to feed themselves on the basis of taking only what one needs. But now the variety of technological needs has turned land for food into land for export crops and mining, or activities that sustain only a few in Africa. The rest must go hungry, their community dehumanized and the earth pillaged and the air polluted. One could sum all this up with the observation that *globalization knows nothing of hospitality.*

African women theologians do not see economic problems as separate from spiritual ones. The inability to render hospitality is a spiritual deficiency. Debt and hunger has strained African hospitality, just as the flight from the farms and the land left rural lands desolate and rural life no longer sustainable. Urban unemployment strains hospitality not only at the point of food and clothing, but also in the lack of a roof over one's head. In traditional hospitality the least one could do was to provide shelter for the night. In urban areas even this is becoming increasingly impossible, what with all the armed robbery and the confidence tricksters. Therefore, Murigande asks: 'What is hospitality in the midst of no housing, slums, neglect of hygiene, criminality, malnutrition, unemployment, delinquency, prostitution and so on?' (1996: 23). Add to this the structural adjustment programs and all of the socio-economic and political contexts in which this theology is being crafted.

These oft-rehearsed changes in Africa work against the practice of hospitality. There is nothing to share but our poverty. But there is more that we are losing in the midst of all this. What have been sacrificed are moral, spiritual and cultural values. African women, like Murigande, posit that our spirituality is to be involved in turning things around and discovering how to insert hospitality into a system that serves profit, and develop a mutation of the market that is also a servant to the civil society and its poor.

Women theologians are not using the word hospitality lightly. They are grappling with its meaning, going into their own and other African languages and cultures to sharpen their understanding of the word. Mirana R. Diambaye, a Malagasy who lives in Senegal, uses the Wolof word *teranga*, which is part of their social morality and means 'welcoming'. *Teranga*, she says has become a state ideology for the hospitality accorded to visiting dignitaries, while beggars swarm the streets of Dakar, crying *Ngiri Allah*—'give in the name of Allah'—to all who pass by (Ravelonolosoa Diambaye 1996: 29). True, almsgiving is one of the five pillars of Islam and begging has become an institution. Children and adolescents, apprenticed to Islamic religious teachers, are expected to learn humility through begging, but many are those who have to glean sustenance from the streets and who are periodically harassed by the police in their attempts to 'clean the streets' especially for the arrival of visiting dignitaries. Diambaye's reflections on hospitality, therefore, link it with justice. She posits that the use of the word *teranga* requires one to develop a spirituality of truth-telling. Traditional *teranga* consisted of a calabash of cold water, a roof over your head. You arrive, introduce yourself, your village, your family, your family history and so on, and then you are accorded *teranga*.

Present-day cities do not honor these practices. Our *teranga* is for people from the outside on whom we are dependent for our participation in global politics and economy. If we could learn self-support maybe we would still have it in our power to be true to ourselves and to traditional *teranga*. According to the tradition all guests are sacred. But now it is the wealthy guests who are sacred and receive *teranga*, the tourists and the Whites. So where is justice when those who truly cannot afford food and roof are denied *teranga*? These questions reflect a meaning of hospitality that is linked with God's compassion, God's year of jubilee, *the great hospitality that moves from charity to justice and solidarity and results in a just development and a world habitable by all*. In Africa, however, it is becoming increasingly clear that governments have abandoned the governed, except for the wealthy. The well-being of the nation is now linked to the well-being of the rich and the women, the majority of whom are among the poor, are left to pick up the pieces with hospitality.

Those who do not do well, including men, return to their mothers or to their maternal villages or the maternal roots. They return to the womb to seek prenatal comfort and security. Globalization is forcing infantilism on Africa and it is women's hospitality that is expected to nurse back the broken spirit of this continent. What women ask for is a corporate effort such as is being offered by voluntary organizations and the so-called 'civil society'. But the critical question remains with us. 'How long will hospitality remain visible in Africa in this context of permanent impoverishment?', asks Rose-Zoe Obianga. Renate Ndayisaba of Rwanda echoes the traditional assertion that hospitality is in the blood of Africans, and yet she is truthful enough to question the meaning of the word in her own country. Rwandans, like other Africans, see it as 'a duty to welcome, feed house and protect the travellers who stop at your door, they become your guests' (Ndayisaba 1996: 45). She points out that 'community and collectivity' was the ancient system and, as such, the challenge in Rwanda is to resist the temptation to define one's circle of hospitality in a narrow way.

This fundamental African value is becoming visible by its absence. And yet Rose-Zoe Obianga says it is exactly in this context of impoverishment, exploitation and uncertainty that we are called not only to exercise hospitality, but also to spread the message of hospitality, with our eyes fixed on Jesus and Mary of the Magnificat. Justine Kahungu (1996: 56), reflecting on the subject, suggests that those who offer hospitality see in the receiver, God, coming down to see and to test how human beings are doing. For this reason all believers in God are ready to extend hospitality to strangers. Kahungu observes from divine–human kinship the love of God, who takes the initiative to offer hospitality to humans (Deut. 26.5-6). Thus, humans are the guests of God, she says. God expands the hearts of human beings to promote life. The belief then is that both givers and receivers of hospitality do so in the name of God.

In the family and among friends and acquaintances it is a way of life. That is why, in the rural areas of Africa, where tradition still holds good, children without immediate parents are automatically taken care of by others. Orphanages and old people's homes are still considered a Western solution that is becoming necessary because of urbanization. Children are still considered an asset to the whole community. They will grow up to contribute to the general good of the community. So says Kahungu and all of traditional Africa. In spite of the affirmation of hospitality on the basis of culture and religion the theological reflection recognizes the fact of human sin, individual and systemic which can corrupt the nation.

Perversion of Hospitality

We began our survey with a story of how 'parasites' often destroy marriages in Africa. Rose-Zoe Obianga describes this dependency syndrome as a *parasitisme infantilisant*. But the most prevalent perversion of hospitality in Africa, which has political and economic implications, is the limitation of hospitality to one's own ethnic group. Africa's conflicts that are ethnic and racial belie the traditional value of hospitality. Apartheid was the quintessence of the absence of hospitality among races and our civil wars and internal conflicts show up the limitations even among peoples belonging to the same nation, or more accurately 'state', as defined by colonial powers. Exclusion on the basis of color, ethnicity, language, social rank and so on has been the subject of justice-oriented theological reflection and, as lack of hospitality, challenges religious anthropology and therefore the theology of creation. So women go to the Bible to see what that context can provide as paradigms for getting back to our one humanity. They find God entreating Israel to be hospitable to strangers, immigrants and sojourners.

Justine Kahungu (1996: 61) finds that of the 47 persons mentioned in the ancestry of Jesus in Matthew's Gospel five were women, and of the five only Mary was not a 'stranger'. She concludes that in God's plan of salvation there are no strangers. She goes on to recall the role 'strangers' play in the Christ story and comes to the conclusion that hospitality that is limited to those near and dear, is far from that of God whose rain is for the good and the evil alike. The example of God's hospitality requires that we move from tribalism and regionalism to universalism, while respecting—and not merely spiritualizing—differences.

Secondly, she goes on to say, 'The wealth that God's hospitality makes available to us is not only the works of our hands and the fruits of the earth: the earth itself, the land and its beauty and its fertility are not only for our generation but is given in perpetuity to us and to the generations to come.' The African worldview, whose sense of the human community spans past, present and future, has no difficulty with this theological assertion. Further, the African worldview does not allow for the annihilation of the earth nor of the human race. Our future is here on earth and therefore we must be concerned with and work for *la sauvegard de toute la creation*.

A critical form of perversion of hospitality has to do with women. A repertoire of Africa's 'shaming songs' is directed towards women who do not know how to welcome their in-laws, never give anything or are too busy to be disturbed by others. Women are expected to be available to all who claim their attention, and their services. Here the intersection of hospitality with sexuality becomes a source of real danger to women's health and well-being.

Hospitality and Sexuality

In the end what we are dealing with, is the hospitality of women that derives from their sexuality. A study that sets out to examine ecological issues through the faith statements that 'The earth belongs to the Lord', and that human beings are keepers of the earth, ended up by facing not so much on humanity's relation to the earth, but on the agency of women in the human community. But this was no derailment. When women have taken seriously their stewardship, they throw themselves into self-giving love in their community. They argue that as God is hospitable to humanity, so women are to all around them or at least should be. As humanity misuses God's generosity and the earth, so women are misused in the human community. As humanity neglects to live in thankfulness for God's hospitality, so women go without the celebration of their self-giving. Remember, says one of the women, only one out of ten lepers returned to say 'Thank you, Jesus.' So women labor without expecting to be held up in an Eucharistic prayer. It is only a stone's throw from the absence of thanksgiving to the perpetration of mindless exploitation.

The regulations that governs female–male relations in some African societies, such as those described by Biasima Lala (1996), ignore the welfare of women and exploit their sexuality. The lists include the following provisions:

- Men who went to the same school of initiation can exchange wives.
- Absent husbands may be replaced by friends appointed by them.
- Brothers, especially twins, can share the duties of being husband to a wife.

- Sterile husbands may appoint surrogates in order to have children (note the scientific process of sperm donation).
- A healer may have sexual relations with his patient.

Other reports say that sometimes, to allay the fury of conquerors, powerful men and divinities, women are offered. They do not offer themselves, neither are they consulted. They have no choice. Chiefs offer male visitors women of honor, to keep them company for the duration of their visit, or even to be taken away as wives (Moyo 1996: 10).[4] This reminds me of Judges 19.[5] These practices have, however, fallen out of favor and instead an attendant or guide is put at the service of an honored guest. The aim of not leaving a person, who is already away from his own people, utterly lonely is thereby achieved.[6]

These, and similar practices, are reported by women in the narrations of their life experiences and from readings of anthropological and sociological literature as well as those from the study of African Religion. The difference is that the women critique this as the diminution of the humanity of the woman and an exploitation of the sexuality of women to the benefit of that of men. For Africans, most of the above have to do with procreation, but also, they are supposed to allow women whose husbands are unavoidably absent—this includes death and impotence—to fulfill their sexual desires in an approved context. This was the response of these communities to the challenge of keeping the sacred nature of the sexual act, since outside marriage, the act is profaned and

4.   Moyo narrates the encounters between the first Jesuit party to visit Zimbabwe, the capital of the old empire of Mwenemotapa in 1560, and the emperor. The emperor received the party as honored guests and sent them 'gifts, gold, cattle, the choice of any of the king's daughters as wife…this gesture of hospitality' to convey the message 'welcome…feel at home'. Father Gonzalo da Silveira refused, claiming that he was after more spiritual things. The emperor felt insulted and wondered whether men who could refuse gifts were really human.

5.   Here I am referring to the tragic violation of hospitality, in that the concubine was gang-raped by the men of the town all night. This resulted in her being murdered by her owner, her body chopped into 12 parts, and terrible revenge being exacted from the Benjaminites.

6.   Grace Wamue (in discussion, 1996) reports that among the Agikuyu, this practice—euphemistically associated with making a bed for a guest—is sometimes resorted to as a form of sperm donation, or providing surrogate fathers for children whose genetic make-up would be that admired by the man who is offering his daughter. She adds, significantly, that the women—wife or daughter—can refuse to make the bed and the guest can also decline the honor.

becomes dangerous not only to the perpetrators, but to the whole community and the earth.[7] Women theologians now count them as a perversion of sexual hospitality and an exploitation of women since in all cases they are not given the choice of decision, only the stance of protest.

Both polygyny, and the rare cases of polyandry, in Africa responds to the above beliefs around sexuality. Lala (1996: 76) reports that among the Lele of DRC, there is provision for a *femme du village*, that is, the collective wife of a known group of men. This, she says, is polyandry and not prostitution. The men are not clients and do not remain anonymous. They are known and the relationship is approved. She reminds us that both prostitution and celibacy as modes of expressing sexuality were unknown in Africa. African women theologians in general have rejected all these forms as incompatible with the dignity of women and not worth including in the idea of hospitality. Over the years these practices have been severely modified or discontinued altogether, mainly because of women's refusal to comply with tradition. A spirituality of resistance inspires them and Western education, which has replaced traditional initiation, and given women a new sense of self-consciousness and economic independence. In addition, the more frequent encounters with the practices of other Africans, and a need to revisit the politics of procreation as distinct from its religious roots, have all fed women's resistance to a life without choices. Women theologians also see Christianity as a factor in this process. The sacredness of sexuality has to do with the sacredness of the whole of a person's humanity and our responsibility to safeguard the divine image which we are, and choice is critical in this respect.

Theologizing hospitality becomes a prophetic duty. It requires the denunciation of the caricaturing of hospitality. On the part of men in power, both in the economic sphere and in sexuality, there is no hesitation to sacrifice women and children for their own promotion or in order to hold on to their advantages, says Lala. It is our general

---

7.   The only instance I know of stating the approval of premarital sex for women is from the report of a field assistant in Nairobi, Reginah Wamui, in 1998, who said, 'Among Akamba, a virgin is taken back to her parents as she is seen as not prepared for a husband.' This suggests that girls are expected to have their first coitus with a man who is not going to be a marriage partner. In fact the report states categorically that 'Akamba make their girls have sex before marriage with a different man' (Maryknoll Institute of African Studies, Summer School 1998).

observation that men, including intellectuals, businessmen and politi-
cians, men in the so-called 'modern sector', and men in the traditional
sector including rulers, healers and cultic functionaries, many of whom
are also highly educated in the Western tradition, revert to African traditional norms when it comes to dealing with women. People who are
models of manhood in our societies and leaders of public opinion, are
often among the guilty ones. Under the circumstances, says Lala, the
women become '*l'holocauste offerte*' as their dignity is sacrificed on the
altars of the husbands' self-interest and egoism. Men do what they want
with women in the name of hospitality and few women are able to resist
sexual hospitality. It is a well known and widespread tradition that when
the Church offers hospitality to strangers, it is women who do the actual
work.

Hospitality as a Lifestyle

There is a spirituality that shines through this practice of hospitality. It a
lifestyle that seeks to respond to the nature of God. Granted, it often
entails sacrifice and suffering, yet women especially want to preserve this
as the only sustainable style of life for humanity. From the constant grappling with women's self-image as nurturers has emerged the need to
revisit the age-old religious concept of sacrifice. It is present in Africa's
three religions and has played a critical role in the collective memories
of several communities. Women's daily experience is that they have to
forgo a lot simply to keep their families fed. The costs of being motherly
in terms of lost opportunities are incalculable. The misuse of the concept
to contain women is a reality, and yet, daily, it is evident that life is sustained by other lives. Touching base with Mama, means touching base
with life, returning to the womb and the breast, back into the security of
being tied to Mama. To meet this expectation, women have had to
tailor their lives and attitudes to fit the role. Is this a conscious self-
giving or simply doing the expected, in order to keep the peace and not
be judged guilty of rebelliousness or of being a renegade? Looked at
from this angle, Njoroge (1996) decries women's self-sacrifice. Her
approach is that women should focus on the life of Christ as a model
and reject the life-denying suffering they undergo or are made to
embrace.

Betty Govinden adds, 'God is salvific only when She can be seen as
suffering with us, who also heals women and empowers them to rise

from the dead and live again beyond the grasp of this destructive violence' (Govinden 1996b: 114). While Njoroge concludes by pointing out that 'A caring and compassionate Jesus travelled the path towards Golgotha, not to perpetuate crucifixion, but to bring them to an end.' Christ, she says 'lives out our call to holistic motherhood', which for me includes ensuring that men, too, honor the path of salvific self-giving which should benefit both self and the whole community of created beings. As it is, our experience is that communities, including churches, are wont to sacrifice women. Women are coerced to sacrifice their charisma, in order to maintain male power. Hence, Hinga (1992: 184-85) writes against the scapegoat-type sacrifice of omen which she labels 'wrongful'.

In the African women's theology, sacrifice is associated with the cross and with suffering. It is counted as vicarious suffering that brings health, healing and life to the other. But the exploitation of women that uses this model, has made pastors like Grace Ndyabahika, point out the problems. When we accept that women are helpers as God is helper, and we claim Christ as our example, we include, of course, the factor of sacrifice in our understanding of God and Jesus. God affirms that God gave up Jesus, who gave up Glory in order to be one of us, a human being. This letting go is an element in sacrifice. What we have failed to do, is to insist that men too are made in the image of God and so must be helpers, nurturers and sustainers *of all that God cares for*. And if this means letting go, so be it! All men and women must empty themselves in sacrifice and for the good of others and the survival of the community (Ndyabahika 1996: 26). This is what Ndyabahika would preach. The Pauline concept of self-emptying is not questioned. It is simply applied to all humans equally. But the counseling from the male pastors, reported by women, suggests that at least in marriage they expect that all the 'letting go' would be done by women only. So then women ask, 'When will women be considered divine without the burden of self-sacrifice, if men can get by without it?'

Njoroge (1996: 12) identifies generosity, mutuality, reciprocity and caring as the central principles of community building in Africa. 'Nurturing relations and righting wrongs are the foundations of African ethics', she says. She argues that since ethics in the African experience, as in Christianity, come from religious beliefs, Christians cannot very easily discard the theology of the cross as a source of ethical norms for Christians. It is the kind of ethical principle we derive from the cross that is being debated. For her, 'the cross is the sign of solidarity, showing how God suffers with us and what it means to suffer with another'. Because of the emphasis on corporate personality, freedom, too, cannot be achieved in isolation, so the story of Jesus, the whole Christ-event, takes place in the midst of community. Jesus and the crowd make up the revelation of God's salvation. Jesus of Nazareth depended on the crowds who followed him, a community that shared his vision, albeit partially, and was brave enough to tell the story. The crowd that announced his entry to Jerusalem, the crowd that gathered in the upper room and the crowd that heard the Pentecost story were all part of the salvation story. Without the crowds that died as Christians and those who watched them die, the story of Jesus may never have been told as salvific. Jesus plus the crowd of men and women, make up the image of God's anointed, the messiah who brings well-being. Women imitating Jesus must bear in mind that the Christ-role is a community enterprise.

In 'Be a Woman and Africa Will Be Strong', Oduyoye argues that women in churches in Africa have made a conscious decision to stay (Oduyoye 1978: 51). Their presence is a deliberate choice not to abandon her, the Church, into the hands of men. This intentional action is therefore a living and life-enhancing sacrifice, because to her mind those who stand in the midst of an oppressive situation in solidarity with all who suffer, offer a positive form of sacrifice. Not all sacrifice is victimization. Conscious self-sacrifice, which is related to resistance, embodies the hope of redemption and may even bring joy to the one who does the 'letting go'. Mary, forgoing a traditional marriage ceremony, did so singing a song that expresses a spirituality of resistance such as African women express when they express themselves counter-culturally over what demeans their humanity. They do reject traditional practices that constitute injustice and are a misuse of religion. A case in point is the *Trokosi* in Ghana, which has nothing of the hope that is present in the self-sacrifice on the cross.[8] When women appropriate the theology of suffering and sacrifice associated with the cross, they are not asking for others to 'make them' take up crosses that they themselves refuse to bear. They are expressing their willingness to do their part in the struggle against evil. They are by their lives making a statement that, to defeat death, we must risk death.

---

8.   *Trokosi* is a system of punishment for crime which provides unpaid labor managing the property attached to religious shrines. There is legislation abolishing the practice.

The challenge of the sacrifice motif comes out of the meaning of suffering, an experience that women live with and respond to. Sacrifice, as a theological paradigm, has to be examined in the economic and socio-political contexts. It cannot be dismissed or simply refused as if it was a device specially constructed by societies to oppress women. What we are faced with is a situation that calls for the sacrifice of various forms and intensities, by all who dwell on earth, the affluent consumer-oriented societies included. For African women, facing sacrifice realistically involves basic daily life issues of survival versus the degree of enhancement of style of life. Who is making the sacrifice? For whom or what is it being made? What is the cost of the sacrifice? Most important for women: is it voluntary, habitual, as in cultural conditioning, or is it deliberately imposed? In this debate, the most important challenge that women have identified is how to get men to mature into the spirit of voluntary sacrifice. For the rest, it is the women's struggle to resist the diminution of their wills and the scope of their choices, which constitute the refusal of dehumanization.

Women face daily survival issues of managing their hearth-holds and they give up their time and energy, muster their ingenuity and creativity to assure life for others. The question some have raised is whether we can label sacrifice, 'that which one does because one cannot do otherwise'. Contemporary experiences demonstrate that even if in the cases when all have been socialized in a particular direction, not all women comply, and not all men refuse voluntary loss in order that others might live. Some have also argued that sacrifice on the part of women is no sacrifice, as they are in fact acting in self-interest, they are protecting their own survival, saving their own faces and avoiding the taunt, blame and ridicule of the society. They do what they do in order to avoid this psychological pain, namely, that African women compromise their personal abilities and integrity. This view highlights the awareness that giving up for the survival of the whole, is incumbent on all, but that women have become the torch-bearers of this way of life. In the final analysis, the difference between being forced by circumstances and conditioning to adopt a sacrifice ideology and choosing to make a decision for self-deprivation, is what the debate is about. This is a decision, not only for African women to make, but also for all of humanity in crises. On our African women's micro-level, what we look for is that we who make sacrifices have to determine its dimensions and extent. We question whether indeed those who are forced to experience loss in the context of Africa's poverty and deprivation could be said to be making sacrifices or shall we say they are victims?

In 'Be a Woman and Africa Will Be Strong' (Oduyoye 1978: 51) and in *Daughters of Anowa* (Oduyoye 1995) Oduyoye tries to call attention to the necessity of making a distinction between making a sacrifice and being sacrificed as a victim. The lines are never too neatly drawn. The appropriation of women's habitual mode of making sacrifices is exploited by religious bodies both for their agenda and their teaching. The Church continues to sacrifice women to the ideology of the family while making only cursory references to husbands about giving up their bodies to save wives and children. The sacrifice motif has also been used by women to turn themselves into salvific figures for their families and communities, but nowhere do they glorify the suffering that is a necessary companion to sacrifice. Anne Nasimiyu (1989: 131) says that women feel worthy when they can sacrifice themselves for others, but she does not thereby approve of the suffering that goes with cultural practices that feed patriarchy and diminishes women. None can reserve the right to sacrifice an unwilling person. It is the unwilling sacrificing of the poor by the rich that has to be resisted.

The language of suffering in African women's theology, is part of the language of life. Children and people in power benefit from socio-economic conditions which they do not directly help to create. For the former, one makes a living sacrifice, but for the latter, the only appropriate response is resistance, the refusal to be victimized. On all levels, from the familial to the global, what women need to insist upon is that *Baanu so a emmia* (when two carry, it does not strain, that is, it is made easier). The unilateral sacrifice by women, whether forced or voluntary, is by itself inadequate to the challenges we face in Africa. The unilateral acceptance of poverty and privations in the Third World is inadequate to the challenges of global warming and other ecological disasters. The only sacrifice that will be life-giving is a systemic sacrifice in which all participate and do so by letting go and sharing power. The theology of sacrifice has to do with the culture of violence, economic, political, social, cultural and religious. It has to do with militarism, oppressive hegemony and the preservation of the deadly status-quo. It has to do with blood-sacrifice and a God who bans human sacrifice but accepts the sacrifice on the cross. It has to do with the Christian commemoration of this event in the Eucharist. But above all it has to do with a sacrifice of praise for life which urges us on to help God sustain life.

Mindless violence has nothing to do with sacrifice. Sacrifice connotes giving life in order to assure life or at least for the sake of assuring life, and is only truly effective if it is conscious and consensual. Thus spousal rape, for example, cannot be said to be done as a sacrifice of the will of the wife, for the sake of having children, an argument I have heard in Africa. What is being highlighted by women like Betty Govinden, is that it is easy to speak of suffering being redemptive while ignoring the causes of it. She continues that human beings cannot turn away, escape from the reality of the pain around us, and look to heavens where there will be neither sighing nor weeping. She uses the lens of South Africa's Land Act, an example of hospitality that is exploited, and which made it possible for men to be forced into cities and mines and on to the farms of white people, as a paradigm of what happens to women in Africa (Govinden 1996b: 115-16). Society makes laws that turn women into slaves in their homes as was the lot meted out to Blacks in South Africa; slaves in the land of their ancestors. This kind of suffering is exploitation, it is suffering that goes to enrich others while the victims are dehumanized. Here there is neither the element of choice nor of mutual enrichment, nor even the joy of seeing others live because you let go.

Christian women in Africa seek fullness of life, but they would also hold the whole body of Christ accountable for the achievement of this goal. If some, women and men, are dedicated to seeking only their own advantage, the objective of the sacrifice cannot be reached. In *Daughters of Anowa* (Oduyoye 1995) Oduyoye calls on men to hold their end of the sacrifice bridge, so that all, especially the weak may cross from dying to living. That is what hospitality calls for.

Chapter Eight

Resurrection of the Body: An Eschatology

The Resurrection of the body is used as the image for dealing with African women's spirituality of hope, because with the coming of women on the theological scene, the disembodied theology that shirks real people's actual experiences has been effectively challenged. The bodies of women entombed behind the stone of patriarchy has appeared to underline the integrity of our humanity and the need for a holistic view of salvation.[1] The new thing promised in Jer. 31.22 has come to mean for us, that women will protect the unity and integrity of humanity. In the Jesus story, it was women who were determined to do honor to the body, who were entrusted with the message of the Resurrection of the body, the message of hope that said, 'death does not have the last word'.

In both Christianity and in African culture, a focus on self is not encouraged, nevertheless ignorance of how our bodies work is unforgivable. It has been the source of many misogynist myths, and we need to shed this primal innocence. Just as we learn the structure and organization of metaphorical bodies like church and speak of what makes for their health and healing, so we must treat our own real bodies. African women have taken a serious look at their own bodies and especially the role that their reproductive parts and functions play in the definition of their personhood. We know that the female body is honored in Africa while it is fecund, for it is the vehicle for ensuring the perpetuity of human life. This has led to attempts to hedge it about, protect it and to make it the property of men who otherwise had no scientific argument

---

1. For the neuroses that accrued to women's bodies, see Armstrong (1996: vii-viii).

for laying claim to their progeny and therefore to the hope of immortality.

The *Resurrection of the body* as in Christianity, is an article of faith derived from the Christ-event together with a general resurrection waiting fulfillment which Christian tradition places as a time when it would please God to bring history to an end. Put side by side with liturgical phrases like 'world without end', 'for ever and ever', 'unto ages of ages', translated into my language as 'to thousands of years' or 'to all days', the notion of a physical end to human existence and to the earth remains unclear. But as an article of faith it regulates the Christian agenda. However, many questions remain unanswered and it is thought best to follow the advice of Jesus and leave it as a mystery. This line of discourse has therefore not appeared on the agenda of African women theologians, whose theology is rooted in the household of God as it is experienced here and now, and as it is to be expected here and now.

The belief taught by African Religion which continues to influence life and death in African thought is that we 'rise from among the dead' through the infants we give birth to. Hence it becomes imperative for all to bring children into this world, and women are seen as having the greater part of this responsibility. The Malawi myth of origins cited above even tells us that in the beginning it was believed that women have children by themselves.[2] The second aspect of women's role in this human duty to perpetuate life is located in her having a body that lactates. This has given rise to women being assigned all kinds of nurturing and caring roles and jobs, even those outside biological motherhood. Thus motherhood and mothering which are prominent in other aspects of women's theology becomes part of the reflections on 'resurrection of the body' (Landman 1996: 100).

Women's hope for the resurrection of the body is also a hope that Christianity will finally come to terms with the fact that we humans are embodied in different forms, but both sexes constitute gifts of God and that women do not have to become men to be human (Armstrong 1996: 169-77, on virgins and martyrs). It is a hope that women themselves will feel fully human in the body God has given them. Thus, women have to come to terms with their particular embodiment. Contemporary challenges to female genital operations, other surgeries to modify other parts of the female anatomy, healthy living regimes, fattening and slimming courses are all evidence of this awareness. An extension to this

2.   See Chapter 5, on 'Being Human'.

resurrection of the body, is the struggle against racism, ethnocentrism and tribalism that women engage in. How African women are perceived as poor Blacks and the suffering slaves of poor Blacks, the stereotypes that go with these images, the refusal of others to see the complexity in woman-being in Africa—these are all being confronted with the positive and empowering image of God made human, a particular person in a particular culture. Demonizing and dismissing Africans only fuels the anger that kindles African women's resistance. They show by what they do and say that God can inhabit a human body, sharing the burdens of Africans, women and men. The resurrection of the body further reminds us that although it is what we are, and not our bodies that are in the image of God, God needed a body to experience fully human life as we know it.

Fullness of Life

Traditional hope for fullness of life is described by the Akan as the gift of graces which include having all one's faculties in a functioning order, health, procreation, prosperity, victory, rain for the removal of evil, and harmony with nature. Africans are at home in life when they can cele-brate life. With Christianity promising fullness of life, women have stuck closely to churches in the hope that as the body of Christ, the Church, by God's grace and the power of Jesus, will meet their need through its ministrations; if not now, then in the near future. Women never say 'never': when it has to do with the good expected of life, what they say is 'not yet'. Hence hope has become another critical theme in African women's theology. The eschatology they find relevant and empowering is a theology of hope.

In her article, 'The Alchemy of Risk and Hope', Denise Ackerman describes hope as

> part of the fibre of our humanness, it is creative expectation. It is our human response to evil, adversity and destruction and it claims account-ability from The One who holds out promises of justice, peace and wholeness. Hope is our refusal to accept defeat and to live for what we hope for. We act on our hope because we know we have to make our hope happen. This she says is why women wrestle with all that is dis-empowering, wait with patience and endurance for the fullness of New life that will be ushered in because they refuse to give in to death, to hopelessness and to apathy (Ackermann 1996b: 144).

Women give of themselves because they believe that giving ensures life and preserves the life-force, face and dignity of others. They hope that maintaining the tradition of sharing as a communal responsibility will teach reciprocity which brings peace, prosperity and blessedness to all. In contemporary Africa this aspect of African culture which is reinforced by the gospel, is also the most challenged by modernization on the pattern of the West. Westernization of Africa together with poverty has undermined the African principle of reciprocity. Hospitality is taken for granted and exploited. Women's continued adherence to these values is a stance of 'in spite of' anchored in the hope of Resurrection. They re-tell again and again the story of the three women who set out to anoint the body of 'the crucified one', knowing full well that there was a colossal stone to be rolled away before they could reach the body. Not even Africa's mammoth poverty can breed despair in women even though from the outside what others see is a future of 'pain, death, the misery of watching one's children die and the death of hope itself'.[3] The death of hope' is an impossible concept in African women's theology, because they believe the Scripture that says, with God, they can scale walls (Ps. 30).

Women's theology faces squarely Africa's poverty because women are the ones doubly affected. Their vision of God's will as *shalom, alafia* (Yoruba), *amani* (kiSwahili) by which we mean peace and prosperity for Africa, does not allow for despair. Women's theology of hope is one that denounces as outside the will of God, all their experiences of oppressive cultural beliefs and practices, hunger, disease and injustice. God does not intend Africans to be wretched. When women theologians highlight a spirituality of resistance, they do so out of their refusal to generalize women's tolerance of evil and humiliation and oppression. They know that in every age and every generation there have been women who have refused anonymity and marginalization. The hope is that, as Kanyoro puts it, more and more women will no longer live their lives without determining the course of it, and in anticipation of that day, the women theologians act on that hope. Their call to all women

3.   See Francis Woodie Blackman (1995: 104-105). Here Inga Gibel (Jewish, Zionist, feminist) the women's representative on the American Jewish committee speaking at the end of UN Forum 85, describing the situation of women worldwide, said: 'At the base of the column of despair were the poor, black women of South Africa, Uganda and Ethiopia, where the only future foreseeable was pain, death the misery of watching one's children die and the death of hope itself.'

to reject dehumanization and anonymity arises out of the hope of God's will being done on earth, here and now. If God knows and calls each one of us by name, then we need to respond both as individuals with personal names and as a community that belongs to the household of God.

They believe that there must be some alternative to the lives they live and the hopes and declarations of African women creative writers support them. The dignity of humanity that women believe in, and which they believe is the will of God, has become a ground of hope in women's theology. Hope makes women utilize their anger against unnecessary suffering. They turn anger into compassion as a route to transformation. In women's theology, hope projects more life even when there is no sign of the end of death.

The context of women's theology of hope is aptly illustrated in Emecheta's *Head above Water* (1986) and her *Destination Biafra* (1982). In these writings she asks fundamental questions about women and marriage, the locus of much of African women's limitations, dealing especially with the lack of choice and voice, that women experience in that institution. There are several areas of women's lack of personhood, but the institution of marriage crystallizes the situation. Reaching out for a liberative future, Emecheta, in the critique of marriage, envisions a future in which her 'sons would treat their wives as people, individuals, not like goats that have been taught to talk' (Emecheta 1986: 127). Her images of women who are persons are marked by wealth, industry and independence of mind. Womanhood will also be marked by benevolence. These beautiful women full of sense and understanding could also be excellent wives and mothers but they are not the property of men. She writes: 'My daughters... God help me, nobody is going to pay any bleeding price for them.' Debbie, her main character and the 'new woman' in *Destination Biafra*, refuses to be advertised like a fatted cow. She would not go into a marriage of unequals in which, before long, she would not have any image of her own. She did not want to see herself marrying a rich man and breeding till menopause (Emecheta 1982: 44, 113, 117). In *The Joys of Motherhood* she produces a court scene in which women are made aware that their husbands do not own them (Emecheta 1979: 218).[4] Here we find the hope for a resurrection of women's

4.   Many Africans from patrilineal groups argue that the economic factors (gold, cows, money) that pass from the groom's family to the bride's does not constitute 'buying a woman'. It goes to replace the services that the natal family had lost in

bodies from the status of flesh that is possessed, to an integral part of their being as human beings in the image of God, having a will and able to respond with creativity to their environment. When this image has been raised from the tomb of patriarchal marriage, we shall begin to hear even more clearly visions of fullness in other areas of life.

The Hope of Transformation

> ...unconditional obedience to the will of men and their whims was something against which many women instinctively rebelled, despite having been through ritual school. But that rebellion had an enormous cost...yet I was prepared to bear the cost, if the price I paid resulted in my becoming, the strong independent woman I knew I could be, and longed to become. I yearned to be a liberated woman who needs a man for the right reasons—reasons of friendship, mutual respect and support, trust, reciprocal dependence, and love which, in going beyond mere sex and childbearing, encompassed the feelings and the soul. I knew I had the potential to become such a woman, despite what I had been through and the world in which I lived (Mathabane 1994: 213).

These words of a South African woman could have come from the writings of many women theologians who hope for the transformation of the relationships between women and men in Africa, and reflects much of what one reads from women creative writers of Africa.

Women are struggling for justice and participation also in church and society and they project into the present what they envision to be the ethos of the household of God, where all talents are developed and put at work for the good of the whole community and the dignity of each individual. Here none is excluded and inferiority and superiority become inappropriate concepts. The concept of *koinonia* which is used in the ecclesiology, is exegeted to picture what it would mean if women could live their lives as daughters rather than doormats in the church, using their skills as they feel called instead of being told where they may or may not contribute. The resurrection of the Church, the body of Christ, will depend on the full participation of women who are spelling out

---

sending her into another family. The affinal family is therefore compensating for this gain. If this is not a 'sale', I fail to understand it, especially as it is not the one rendering services who gets the compensation. Women who approve of this practice claim it is a demonstration that they are valued by their natal families. See *Daughters of Anowa* (Oduyoye 1995: 133-34) for the matrilineal explanation.

afresh the mission of the Church and challenging traditional imagery of what constitutes power and authority.

Women hope for a transformed Church, because in Africa, the Church remains an institution with a potential for contributing to bringing in the new life that women struggle for. The hope of resurrection is what inspires women's spirituality of resistance and persistence characterized in the creative writings cited above. Women's resistance to anonymity and dehumanization encompasses not only their own humanity but that of all who are marginalized or oppressed or overlooked, as well as a hope for the redemption of the humanity of those who do the oppressing and the marginalizing. The hope for a community of women and men around God's table, is what anchors this theology.

The Anchors of Hope

Hope is kept alive by women in the face of poverty, because the God of the Magnificat is believed to be a living God who is doing a new thing, making a new world and a new humanity that will live with the justice and peace, the freedom of the new creation. Women find hope in the ideals of African culture, in spite of the aspects that have become obstacles to the quality of life in Africa. The hope is anchored on the fact that the empowering elements of community building in biblical experience are also found in Africa. Women find in the Bible communities that are theistic, subscribe to the dignity of the individual as created by God and God's image. They find in the Bible communities that believe in justice and in caring for its own as well as for strangers. Several images of community in the Greek Bible correspond to what traditional Africa was keen to achieve. Women theologians affirm that these things shall be. Women hope to rescue the family from patriarchy, hospitality from abuse and lack of reciprocity, and the community spirit from the atomization of society and excessive individualism.

Women hope for a transformed church that will promote the tenets of community that served Africa's harmony. All this is firmly anchored in their faith that 'Christ is sent by God to an alienated world where the presence of God takes the shape of the Crucified One'. Suffering, death and ultimate victory is the lesson from the life of God on earth. In Christ we see the one who is perfect suffering and dying because of the promise of resurrection, which is God's ultimate victory over this world's alienating forces and which opens a future for a new humanity

(Nasimiyu 1989: 131). The acts of hope in Africa flow from the belief that though there is judgment at the end of life in African Religion, Christianity and Islam, even here and now we are being judged by what we do and by our commitment to the unveiling of the reign of God. We are called to hope because of the transforming power of God. It is hope which sustained the independence and anti-apartheid struggles in Africa. Hope sustains the struggle for better life, hope keeps us committed and active. Hope accompanies our struggle for the recognition of women's full humanity as we seek to dismantle negative cultural conditioning and demands.

The eschatology of women puts the accent on what they see in the Bible as the future of God, the new creation found in the risen Christ. Biblical and life experiences confirm the hope of transformation, a hope for the world and confidence in God is able to bring about the transformation that is needed. Hope springs out of the belief that what is, is not what must necessarily remain, and it is certain to change if it does not conform to God's future. They point out that, though we are created in the image of God, we are still in the process of becoming who we are, hence the action to transform what does not contribute to the ambience of the household of God.

Women are acting on modern marital and property laws after years of silence, owing to the fear of losing face. They hope and work so that new procedures will be evolved to bring equity into this area of life as the system becomes more gender-sensitive. The responses to traditional socialization are directed by a hope for change in the direction of justice, putting things right. Women speak out on practices in African Religion that amount to the torture and enslavement of women even when they risk being ostracized. Women speak out on theological interpretations, especially of sin: they analyze the economy, they discuss power and empowerment and participate in justice-making, taking risks in hope of new life. The confidence that Christianity has resources for the transformation of dehumanizing culture is based on events in the life of Jesus, who had challenged tradition and acted on the side of justice and compassion. It is by the values entrenched in our understanding of God's future, that women keep hope alive. The hoped-for household of God is a house for all peoples. African women's stance has been that their liberation is bound up with the liberation of the communities in which they live. They have sought to bring men along in the struggle to highlight women's lives. Women have accepted sacrifice as a community need and have argued that, for the health and peace of the whole community both men and women should be ready to let go of something for the mutual benefit of the community. They base this approach on the sacrifice made by Jesus and the promise of resurrection and of God's ultimate victory over the alienating forces of our world. All will be well, but it will take the sacrificing of inordinate self-interest by both men and women.

Women's condoning of wrongs, silence over oppression and taking on all the sins of the community are denounced as non-salvific. Self-sacrifice is either for all or for no one. It does not work out as God's method of salvation if victimization is being labelled as self-giving. What will open a future for the actualization of the new humanity is the total participation of the entire community in the restoration of harmony and the bringing about of shalom, peace and prosperity. The link between crucifixion and resurrection is expounded by Nasimiyu, but I would insist further, that the Christ-event calls both men and women to the twin experience of cross and resurrection. The cross teaches the resistance of evil, but hope goes beyond the cross to its God-ordained denouement. We risk sacrifice and cross, we struggle against evil and endure many scars, because armed with hope we already see life defeating death. African women have taken the risk to sacrifice for the good of all in their hearth-hold, church and society, in the hope that the new life will result; they have sustained life, but to move to the new, the call goes out to all. Women sustain the hope that more and more people will hear this call to the future. In Ackermann's paper she writes, 'risk, hope and struggle are intertwined in a relationship of synergy' (Ackermann 1996b: 143). Risk and hope, she says, are inseparable, because to hope is to risk and both demand a commitment to struggle and sustain them. Women who risk voluntarily, do so for the sake of justice and as an act of calculated resistance that there may be a future for the new that God is bringing in.

Resurrection for Humanity

Women of faith—like men of faith—want to live a life of resurrection, a new life, given through their encounter with Jesus…[women] experienced the welcome to the newness of resurrection (Kanyoro 1996b: 159).

The experience of the resurrection of Jesus has been the source of empowerment for the resurrection of women's bodies, which has in turn knit together once more the integrity of women's humanity. It breaks the hedges that limit the flowering of the fullness of life in and for themselves. Resurrection of the body is the motif for reviewing women's theology of transformation and of the victory of life over death. Resurrection does not wait for a physical end of the world, but happens any time new life in Christ is experienced.

Women's theology goes to the Bible not only to locate the scenes of oppression, but to show that they are sinful and against the will of God. Each new reality that they encounter leads them to interpret the word of God anew, to act on the word so as to change that reality, convinced that through their action God will bring about the new that is in tune with God's will. The liberation theology of African women underlines the hope in Yahweh that they find in the Hebrew Bible. It underlines the expectation that God will hear our cries and would come to our rescue. This is what keeps women going. From the Greek Bible they see their hope in Jesus' preaching of the coming reign of God and the signs of its presence among us even here and now. The *kindom* is not only coming, 'See, it is here already!'—and this faith sprouts the hope in the resurrection, every time wickedness is defeated by beneficence, and benevolence marks our attitudes towards the other. By every effort to bring a little smile into a situation of doom, faith is strengthened that life will defeat death, and that injustice will flee the presence of justice. Women live in the knowledge that the tyranny of patriarchy is bound to end. Because biblical hope tells of a time without death and tears, because God is the God of life and Jesus has promised abundant life, the suffering of women cannot be the last word. There must be a resurrection in its wake—new life, love, peace and justice—a new creation, a new community, the household of God in which all things are made new.

Chapter Nine

The Way Forward

Where is the way forward
When we do not want to know where we are
When we do not care where we've come from
When we refuse to talk about where we would like to be
or where we want to head for?
How do we know which is the way forward?[1]

Working on these issues with African women for close to two decades, I often felt like concluding that we are lost, if we refuse to face the reality of our changing world. Lost, because the hierarchical patriarchal world, with its marginalization and privileged positions, is fast eroding and, therefore, cannot support the many exploitative structures that we used to take for granted. Sexism has had its day and Christian theology, that has perpetuated it with its history of 'neuroses' regarding human sexuality, has a responsibility to play a more positive role. Religion has what it takes to do this. It is for this reason that this final reflection bears the title 'The Way Forward'. What is being said here is that, there has to be a way forward. There is a hymn, which assures us that led by God's unerring Spirit, we shall not stray in the desert nor miss our providential way (an excerpt and paraphrase from hymn 608, Methodist Hymnbook, 1933). It is this faith that accompanies African women theologians in their search for a dynamic theology and spirituality. Further, we as

1.   The poem is the author's own, inspired by Williams (1993: 122): 'Making a way where there is not way' and Armstrong (1996: 310): 'It should be possible for us to use those (empowering) aspects of our heritage to carry us a long way forward'. The book by Armstrong (1996) is described by the publishers as 'a passionate and provocative interpretation of the history of women in Christianity—a history blighted by the neuroses of a patriarchal western culture'. This culture has become the heritage of colonial and Christian Africa as well.

women in theology are not alone in this hope. Other women–centered thinkers are also seeking 'the way forward'. For 'our stories', therefore, we review here the supportive evidence from Nigerian women creative writers.

Chikwenye Ogunyemi sums up the debates on the African women's search for liberation as follows:

> The Palava is not whether people should be liberated, for that point is taken for granted by writers' courage in tackling different manifestations of oppression of women and men and children. The moot points are how to free the children from the trauma of racism and ethnicism; stem the terror of militarism, totalitarianism, and political chaos, tackle the poverty engendered by international economics, and *eliminate the waste in human resources resulting from sexism* (Ogunyemi 1996: 330; my emphasis).[2]

This is the agenda of African women as Ogunyemi distills it from their writings. Like the theologians these women in literature are for the integral liberation of Africa that takes care of the entire lives of women, children and men. The same agenda will be found in the autobiography of Eva Chipenda, of Angola (Chipenda 1996). Like the creative writers, Chipenda is not afraid to tell the truth about what sexism has meant in her life. In her story we find an illustration of what Ogunyemi has observed about the lives of African women from the creative writers and the theologians will agree that:

> Women tried to bear whatever they experienced in their fathers' houses and later in their husbands' because it was impolitic, sometimes forbidden, to mention unspeakable experiences, though women have always tried to share such experiences if only with limited audiences (Ogunyemi 1996: 120).

Today, much is in the open for us to critically examine and to take counsel in order to transform into a more humanized community. This 'truth-telling with regard to sexism' is replacing the traditional coping devices, which Ogunyemi describes as 'this female heritage of occasional defiance, complicity, grumbling, secrecy, silence, conformity, submitting and unwitting collusion with the male.' These devices, as she rightly

---

2.   I am indebted to Dr Ogunyemi for the possibility of making connections with this genre of women's writings in this concluding chapter. Searching for a representative work to compare with the theological efforts, I found this the most critical review of the state of the art of African women's creative writings. In addition, my Nigerian experience enables me to appreciate and appropriate her thinking.

observes, 'have perpetuated gross misbehavior by men' (Ogunyemi 1996: 120).

What has religion to say to this experience of women? What is the way forward, if the curse of sexism is to be removed? Nigeria is my second home and the place that jolted me from naive asexual approach to human relations. 'All men are equal' for me meant all women and all men are to be treated to justice and equity. 'All fingers are not equal' meant co-operation, each doing its specific part according to its gifts. I operated from a private paradise where being male or female was not the reason for getting on in life, and where people are enabled to develop and contribute their skills to better the common wealth. When I woke up, I became a 'feminist', a person who takes women's lives, women's words, women's experiences, women's writings and women's wisdom, as a cardinal part of a heritage to be appropriated, one who sought out other women so that together we might be strong enough to make our contributions as women to a world that has been hijacked by men. I never lost sight of the fact that a bird with one wing cannot fly and that the foot that stays to crush another cannot move either. I advocated the conversion of men towards communality and inclusiveness. Maybe that makes me a womanist but a discussion of the shades of woman-centeredness is not a key concern of this volume. After twenty years of my first conscious experience of patriarchy in operation, I am asking myself, and others involved in the search for viable and empowering communities, 'Which is the way forward?'

For this, I return to the creative writings of African women as the context for my theological reflection, bearing in mind that, for most Africans in West Africa, and especially in Ghana and Nigeria, the 'nuclear family' consist of the 'hearth-hold', a concept developed by Felicia Ekejuiba, who describes it as a woman and all who eat from her cooking place. The hearth-hold, as she accurately asserts, is the smallest unit in the social structures of Africa. In this unit 'women perceive their responsibilities and role as both catalysts and full beneficiaries of development' (Ekejuiba 1995: 49-54). This observation confirms what many proverbial sayings assert that, 'the survival of many and their spiritual rock is found where mother is'. Hence the concept of mother-ing that I have used in other places. African women who write novels, short stories, plays and poetry are calling for a recognition and integra-tion, which most men writers were at the outset reluctant to give. Some would not even deign to read what we write. This is a women-centered approach to community well-being. Most of these women would not call themselves feminists as that concept has generated images of individualism and middle-class ethos, falsely, I think. More serious indeed is the disavowal based on the non-critique of racism and economic exploitation and spite of Blacks by Whites as well as the Sarah–Hagar syndrome: hence Chikwenye Ogunyemi says, in feminism, 'all the women are white or passing' (Ogunyemi 1996: 108).

The above context is what has caused African women theologians to focus on God's hospitality and human response. From the vantage point of the 'hearth-hold', they see God in the mother role and the Church, indeed the whole society as the hearth-hold of God. They confirm the privilege of the weak in the community, as well as the need to appreciate and utilize their gifts. Do not the Akan say, '*Abofra kawa na enko opayin na nye n'aduan a?*' (An adult cannot wear the ring of a child but a child's food is a different case.) There is no one who can make no contribution to the life of a community. Women's appropriation of their context therefore issues from this fact as well as the faith and hope that spurs them on to transformative actions. Both the dialoguing and the praying are sources of theology that seeks to make strife redundant.

African women theologians are expanding the parameters of theological reflection in Africa as they deepen the meaning of traditional theological motifs and seek to make religious discourse a source of spirituality for life. They are, therefore, making their own contribution to the development of African Christian theology as well as participating in the global woman-centered theology. It seems to me, however, that many would feel at home with the African-American 'womanism', the wise precocious young woman, indeed girl, who wants to get involved and actually does have something to offer.[3] The Asante would call such a girl an *aperewa* and try to curb her spirits. African culture does that to women all the time until one becomes an *aperewa*, seasoned with age and experience with 'a mouth that eats salt and pepper', as Ama Ata

---

3. In 1984 Alice Walker of the United States gave women of African descent the term 'womanist' which she defines as the character of being a woman who is 'precocious, courageous and serious'. Ogunyemi expands this to mean a woman who questions all, who has a community orientation, and subscribes to communalism, who seeks dialogue, palaver in West African parlance. Palaver is a dialogue in which 'the destiny of distressed peoples can be urgently discussed in a meaningful context to avert disaster, not just to talk abstractly' (Ogunyemi 1996: ch. 2).

Aidoo would describe her; a person whose word cannot be ignored (Aidoo 1970).[4]

African women want to put their mouth into familial, ecclesial and national affairs, irrespective of their age. Not only that, they also want to be in on the implementation stage. The comprehensive nature of their discourse fits the mold of the womanist parameters. On the other hand, as Chikwenye Ogunyemi notes, naming is a political matter. We Africans are always being named, our 'bi-racial personal names', the names of our cities and rivers, our lakes and waterfalls; so now we are expected to name ourselves after one or other of the self-named groups. These 'auto-nomous' women are able to do so because they are using their mother-tongue. If African women-centered women name themselves feminists or womanists it should not be understood as imitation or as political alliance with one group or the other. We are signifying the handicap of the linguistic complexity of our context. The way forward proposed by women creative writers, as distilled by Chikwenye Ogun-yemi, form the contexts of the following reflections: they may be label-led womanist for convenience and also to reflect the fact that we all have to indulge in *mperewasem*[5] to save this continent from pre-mature aging, decline and death.

Chikwenye dedicates her book 'To all those past and present, im-mersed in the struggle for Nigerian Freedom.' This I beg to extend to Africa's freedom. She reviews the works of eight Nigerian women novelists: Flora Nwapa, Adaora Ulasi, Buchi Emecheta, Funmilayo Fakunle, Zynab Alkali, Eno Obong, Ifeoma Okoye and Simi Bedford, and with references also to Ghana's Ama Ata Aidoo and Egypt's Nawal El Saadawi and South Africa/Botswana's Bessie Head and others. These women she designates as 'griottes'—women who take on the role of 'entertainer, teacher, social critic, ideologue, and wise but despised mother'.[6] Three of them Flora, Adaora, Buchi were, like myself born, in

4.   This is the designation she gives the Old Man and the Old Woman. In the drama they serve as a chorus, making statements that give cultural and religious explanations to events in other people's lives, especially that of the protagonist, Anowa.

5.   *Mperewasem* is how the Akan describe the words and acts of an *aperewa*. See p. 123.

6.   Ogunyemi creates a feminine form of the French word *griot*. She explains: 'since *griots* are traditionally male or female', she coins the feminine form in French to counter the usual suppression of the feminine when African languages are trans-lated into European idiom (Ogunyemi 1996: 3).

the 1930s and, therefore, are portraying our common experience of colonialism, westernization and Christianization. They speak also of how African womanhood fared in their 'Girls Boarding Schools', as well as how a class of women traders participated in the colonial economy as evidenced by the now famous 'Market Women'.

Ogunyemi weaves a convincing *Aso ebi* (family cloth) of what she calls 'A Womanist Ideology'. My concern as a theologian is this: what is the spirituality that has created this ideology and what is the religious faith that nourishes it? Does religion in fact have a role to play in the way forward? Or rather, what role will religion play in the way forward? The 'resurrection of the body' as a theological motif might stimulate our future reflection as we respond to Africa's agenda—which for the African 'griottes' covers the well-being of all of Africa—but remains women-centered. African women follow a reorientation that hopefully leads from the impasse of individualism, to the traditional community spirit. The griottes' orientation is summed up by Ogunyemi as 'African womanist ideology'. In this she includes 'African women's inclusive mother-centered ideology with its focus on caring, familial, communal, national and international dimensions. Not only is sexism a problem: other oppressive sites includes totalitarianism, militarism, ethnicism (post) colonialism, poverty, racism, and religious fundamentalism.' These issues, she says, must be addressed, as ignoring them is problematic. The women theologians of The Circle will agree with her that there are issues to be thrashed out in the palaver. This is a way forward for it will offset future palaver. African feminism's advocacy of palaver as a methodology is a way forward. We must talk about these things in community, propose and act on solutions as a community of women and men. Ogunyemi cites Katherine Frank as saying, 'African women write about women but do not give us a world without men' (Ogunyemi 1996: 114-15).

Many see the ideology of complementarity, as necessary for 'co-existence while the palaver is still on or when it is over'. African women do not perceive their men as the enemy. They criticize heavily the patriarchal ethos of marriage in Africa, but they still leave room for dialogue (Ogunyemi 1996: 114-15). The suggestion here is that for a way forward we must honor 'the maternal spirit of compromise and inclusiveness'. Ama Ata Aidoo's feminism includes 'believing that African women must have the best that the environment can offer'. She requires that Africans should take charge of Africa, its wealth, its peoples' lives, our own development...' Like her, other African women writers do not limit themselves to matters of gender, comments Ogunyemi (1996: 116). The way forward therefore is for women and men of Africa to put Africa, nation and people before profit and making money out of politics and adversity. It is the mothering ideology that puts the weakest first that should guide our way forward.

The important thing for women of Africa is not whether we are feminists, womanist or 'benign women', communist, socialist or capitalists. What is important is creating an atmosphere, a culture in which our human dignity will become a non-negotiable fact. In this, as in other aspects of Africa's development, the way forward is to name ourselves, to make a contribution to world culture. The way forward that women advocate, is to find our contribution from our African culture, cleared of all that demeans our humanity, especially that of women. We the women-centered women do not want to wait till things go wrong and then protest. We want to be at the ground-breaking sites so that our input can be at the foundations of whatever will be constructed. That we believe is the way forward.

Certainly the way forward does not include pandering to men for fear of reprisals, nor to take on the attitude of 'men-pleasers' (*mmayin anyiso*), but to involve men, in order to 'prevent the palaver from degenerating into a monologue or an unproductive shouting march' (Ogunyemi 1996: 117). So for Africa's women creative writers, the way forward is to promote 'the traditional ideology of collaboration and complementarity. Since dialogue is the style, Ogunyemi quotes Ogundipe-Leslie, another Nigerian woman literary critic who, in writing on the 'fates of African Women in Society', points to the various forms of oppression, namely the fates of children, men, communities, nations and continents that have been raped and remain disoriented from continued sacking and pillaging by rapacious people and their local underlings' (Ogunyemi 1996: 118). In so doing she calls the whole international politico-economic world into the arena of the African woman's palaver.

So then, what is the African woman theologian's contribution to the palaver and its search for the way forward? What is the task of Christianity and Christian theology in this crisis of women seeking, yes, demanding to direct attention to the state of affairs that oppress us all? The 'feminism' that some of us dread so much is in Africa seeking to point to and to begin to step on the way forward. For African women in religion, as for the novelists, the way forward in Africa lies in togetherness, complementarity and harmony. But I personally do not speak of a togetherness, which is based on the muzzling of the other. The Fanti lyric says *Wɔmma me nkasa na gyrema da maanum?* (Let me speak, for I have a tongue in my mouth). I do not speak of a complementarity that allows one to dictate my role; neither do I subscribe to the harmony that is imposed by silencing discordant voices. No, the way forward is more taxing than that. I do not accept the interpretation of variety demonstrated by the five fingers on a hand as nature's endorsement of hierarchy and class; rather it is nature's icon of collaboration and mutuality. Ogunyemi who summarizes the griottes puts her accent on 'flexibility, maturity, maternal disposition, steadfastness of purpose and all-inclusiveness' as the way forward.

All this calls for women who love other women and 'do not hand them over to be crucified because of men'. This constitutes a trap for all on the margins of power, and is, therefore, a road block on the way forward. The way forward is impeded for us in Africa by the 'fear woman' mentality. We are yet to understand that if a lot of women name marriage as a problematic space and the locus of men's oppression of women, they do the community a service, for spousal violence is a debilitating syndrome and patriarchy is the culture in which it grows and thrives.

The way forward is to evoke our cultural heritage of women's strength and live by our non-gender specific pronouns and the naming of women after men and men after women, thus de-emphasizing gender as a binding parameter. The women writers of Africa are shaking African countries out of their complicity. They call for dialogue about everything. For the women in religion this includes women's presence in synods and in church cabinets. They want to 'engage in critical discussion without violating one another'. And we in religion seek to do the same without preconditions entrenched in particular traditions. This is the African women-centered agenda to which The Circle's women-centered theology must respond, critique and inspire.

Bibliography

Ackermann, Denise

    1996a   'Participation and Inclusiveness among Women', in Kanyoro and Njoroge 1996: 136-48.

    1996b   'The Alchemy of Risk, Struggle and Hope', in Mary John Mananzan *et al.*, *Women Resisting Violence: A Spirituality for Life* (Maryknoll, NY: Orbis Books, 1996): 141-46.

Ackermann, Denise, Jonathan A. Draper and Emma Manshini

    1991   *Women Hold up Half the Sky: Women in the Church in South Africa* (Pietermaritzburg: Cluster Publications).

Ackermann, Denise, and Tahira Joyner

    1996   'Earth-Healing in South Africa', in Ruether 1996: 121-34.

Adu-Ampoma, Letitia

    1996   'Divine Empowerment of Women in Africa's Complex Realities' (Circle Conference, Nairobi).

Agumba, Elizabeth

    1997   'The Search for my Place in Society', in Oduyoye 1997: 154-55.

Aidoo, Ama Ata

    1970   *Anowa* (London: Longmans Drumbeat).

Amoah, Elizabeth, and Mercy Amba Oduyoye

    1988   'The Christ for African Women', in Fabella and Oduyoye 1988: 35-46.

Amoah, Elizabeth (ed.)

    1997   *Where God Reigns: Reflections on Women in God's World* (Accra: Samwoode Publishers).

Armstrong, Karen

    1996   *The Gospel According to Woman* (London: HarperCollins/Fount).

Assaad, Marie

    1986   'Reversing the Natural Order', in Pobee and von Wärtenberg-Potter 1986.

Beier, Ulli (ed.)

    1966   *Origin of Life and Death: African Creation Myths* (Ibadan: Heinemann).

Bennet, Bonita

    1986   'A Critique on the Role of Women in the Church', in Itumeleng J. Mosala and Buti Tlhagale (eds.), *The Unquestionable Right to be Free* (Maryknoll, NY: Orbis Books, 1986): 169-74.

Blackman, Francis Woodie

    1995   *Dame Nita: Caribbean Woman, World Citizen* (Kingston, Jamaica: Ian Randall).

Chipenda, Eva de Carvalho
    1996   *The Visitor* (Geneva: WCC Risk Books).

Chukwuma, Helen
    1989   'Positivism and the Female Crisis: The Novels of Buchi Emecheta', in Henrietta Otokunefor and Obiageli Nwodo (eds.), *Nigerian Female Writers* (Oxford: Malthouse Press): 2-18.

Edet, Rosemary
    1991   'A Language of Endearment: A Valuable Asset for Women and Theology', in Edet and Umeagudosu 1991: 37-42.

Edet, Rosemary, and Margaret A. Umeagudosu (eds.)
    1991   *Life, Women and Culture: Theological Reflections* (Lagos: African Heritage Research and Publications).

Ekejuiba, Felicia I.
    1995   'Down to Fundamentals: Women-centred Hearth-holds in Western Africa', in Deborah Fahy Bryceson (ed.), *Women Wielding the Hoe: Lessons from Rural Africa for Feminist Theory and Development Practice* (Oxford and Washington, DC: Berg Publishers, 1995): 47-57.

Ekeya, Bette
    1986   'Woman, For how Long Not?', in Pobee and von Wärtenberg-Potter 1986: 59-67.
    1988   'A Christology from the Underside', in K.C. Abraham (ed.), *Voices from the Third World* (Colombo: EATWOT): 17-29.
    1994   'Motherhood: Avenue for Theological Expression', in Pobee 1994: 99-115.

Emecheta, Buchi
    1974   *Second-Class Citizen* (London: Alison and Busby).
    1977   *The Slave-Girl* (London: Alison and Busby).
    1979   *The Joys of Motherhood* (London: George Breziller).
    1982   *Destination Biafra* (London: Alison and Busby).
    1986   *Head above Water* (London: Fontana Paperback).

Eneme, Grace
    1986   'Living Stones', in Pobee and von Wärtenberg-Potter 1986: 28-32.

Fabella, Virginia, and Mercy Amba Oduyoye (eds.)
    1988   *With Passion and Compassion: Third World Women's Theology* (Maryknoll, NY: Orbis Books).

Govinden, Betty
    1996a   'The Myth of a Divided Spirituality: Questions of Sexuality and Spirituality in South Africa' (unpublished paper, Circle Conference, Nairobi, 1996).
    1996b   'In Search of our own Wells', in Kanyoro and Njoroge 1996: 112-35.
    1997   'Re-Imaging God', in Oduyoye 1997: 148-50.

Hinfebaar, Hugo F.
    1991   'Bemba-speaking Women of Zambia in a Century of Religious Change', in *Studies in Religion in Africa* (Supplements to the Journal of Religion in Africa; Leiden: E.J. Brill).

Hinga, Teresa
    1992   'Jesus Christ and the Liberation of Women in Africa', in Oduyoye and Kanyoro 1992: 183-94.

Idowu, E. Bolaji
    1975   *African Traditional Religion: A Definition* (Maryknoll, NY: Orbis Books).
James, Rhoda Ada
    1990   'The Scope of Women's Participation in the Church', in Oduyoye and
                Kanyoro 1990: 173-87.
Kahungu, Justine
    1996   'L'Afrique, Terre d'Hospitalité', in Kahungu and Fassinou 1996: 56-70.
Kahungu, Mbwiti, and M. Couthin Fassinou (eds.)
    1996   *Le Canari d'eau fraiche ou L'Hospitalité Africaine* (Lubumbashi: Zaire Editions
                Chemins de Vie).
Kanyoro, Musimbi
    1996a   'Challenges of Feminist Theology to Development Work' (unpublished
                workshop paper; Bread for the World, Stuttgart).
    1996b   'God Calls to Ministry: An Inclusive Hospitality', in Kanyoro and Njoroge
                1996: 149-62.
    1997   'God's Word: Life for All', *USB Bulletin* 178/179: 63ff.
Kanyoro, Musimbi, and Nyambura Njoroge (eds.)
    1996   *Groaning in Faith: African Women in the Household of God* (Nairobi: Acton
                Publishers).
Kialu, Gertrude Tundu
    1990   'Human Sexuality', in Oduyoye and Kanyoro 1990: 80-83.
    1996   'La Prostitution au Zaire', in Kahungu and Fassinou 1996: 137-42.
Kuma, Efua
    1980   *Jesus of the Deep Forest* (Accra: Asempa Press).
Lala, Biasima
    1996   'L'Hospitalité et l'Exploitation de la Femme', in Kahungu and Fassinou
                1996: 71-80.
Landman, Christina
    1996   'A Land Flowing with Milk and Honey', in Kanyoro and Njoroge 1996:
                99-111.
Lartey, Emmanuel
    1993   *African Theology: Inculturation and Liberation* (Maryknoll, NY: Orbis Books).
Lwamba, Nkebi
    1996   'L'Hospitalité Africaine au Zaire', in Kahungu and Fassinou 1996: 35-36.
Machema, Alina
    1990   'Jumping Culture's Fences', in Oduyoye and Kanyoro 1990: 131-35.
Mathabane, Mark
    1994   *African Women: Three Generations* (New York: Harper Collins).
Mazrui, Ali A.
    1986   *The Africans: A Triple Heritage* (Boston: Little, Brown & Co.).
Mbondo, Ebenye
    1996   'Femme Pouvoir, Tu Peux Oser', in Kahungu and Fassinou 1996: 11-12.
Moyo, Ambrose
    1996   *The Risk of the Incarnation* (Geneva: WCC).
Mugambi, J.N.K., and Lautenti Magesa (eds.)
    1989   *Jesus in African Christianity* (Nairobi Initiatives Ltd).

Murigande, Catherine
    1996   'L'Hospitalité Africaine et Economie', in Kahungu and Fassinou 1996: 21-
              28.

Nasimiyu, Anne Wasike
    1989   'Christology and an African Woman's Experience', in Mugambi and
              Magesa 1989: 123-35.
    1991   'Christology and an African Woman's Experience', in Robert J. Schreider
              (ed.), *Faces of Jesus in Africa* (Maryknoll, NY: Orbis Books): 70-84.

Ndayisaba, Renate
    1996   'L'Hospitalite Chretienne au Rwanda', in Kahungu and Fassinou 1996:
              45-46.

Ndyabahika, Grace
    1996   'Women's Place in Creation', in Kanyoro and Njoroge 1996: 23-30.

Njoroge, Nyambura
    1996   'Groaning and Languishing in Labour Pains', in Kanyoro and Njoroge
              1996: 3-15.

Nyajeka, Tumani Mutasa
    1996   'Shona Women and the Mutupo Principle', in Ruether 1996: 135-42.

Obianga, Rose-Zoe
    1996   'L'Hospitalite: Disponibilite a autrui et accueil de ses valeurs', in Kahungu
              and Fassinou 1996: 47-55.

Oduyoye, Mercy Amba
    1976   'And Women, Where Do They Come in?', *A Monograph* (Lagos: Metho-
              dist Church).
    1978   'Be a Woman and Africa Will Be Strong', in Letty Russell *et al.* (eds.),
              Inheriting our Mothers' Gardens: Feminist Theology in Third World Perspective
              (Westminster: John Knox Press, 1978): 33-55.
    1984   'Absoluteness of Christ in the Context of Muslim Claims: The Nigerian
              Case', *Orita: Journal of Religious Studies* 16.1 (June).
    1986   *Hearing and Knowing* (Maryknoll, NY: Orbis Books).
    1988   *Who Will Roll the Stone Away?* (Geneva: WCC, Risk Books).
    1989a   'An African Woman's Christ', in EATWOT, *Encounter* 1989: 119-24.
    1989b   'Poverty and Motherhood', *Concilium* 226: 23-30.
    1989c   'The African Family as a Symbol of Ecumenism', *One in Christ* 3: 238-54.
    1995   *Daughters of Anowa: African Women and Patriarchy* (Maryknoll, NY: Orbis
              Books).

Oduyoye, Mercy Amba (ed.)
    1997   *Transforming Power: Women in the Household of God: Proceedings of the Pan-
              African Conference of The Circle 1996* (Accra: Sam-Woode Publishers).

Oduyoye, Mercy Amba, and Musimbi Kanyoro (eds.)
    1990   *Talitha Qumi* (Ibadan: Day Star Press).
    1992   *The Will to Arise* (Maryknoll, NY: Orbis Books).

Ogunyemi, Chikweni Okonjo
    1996   *African Wo/man Palava: The Nigerian Novel by Women* (Chicago: University
              of Chicago Press).

Okure, Teresa
    1992   'The Will to Arise: Reflections on Luke 8:40-56', in Oduyoye and Kan-
              yoro 1992: 221-30.

Pobee, John S. (ed.)
    1992   *Exploring Afro-Christology* (Frankfurt: Peter Lang).
    1994   *Culture, Women and Theology* (Delhi: ISPCK).
Pobee, John S., and B. von Wärtenburg-Potter (eds.)
    1986   *New Eyes for Reading* (Geneva: WCC).
Ravelonolosoa Diambaye, Mirana
    1996   'Dakar: Teranga et Encombrements Humains', in Kahungu and Fassinou 1996: 29-32.
Ruether, Rosemary Radford (ed.)
    1987   *Christology and Feminism* (Lecture, Hiram College, Ohio).
    1996   *Women Healing Earth: Third World Women on Ecology, Feminism and Religion* (Maryknoll, NY: Orbis Books).
Souga, Teresa
    1988   'The Christ-Event from the Viewpoint of African Women: A Catholic Perspective', in Fabella and Oduyoye 1988: 22-29.
Swart, Angelina
    1990   'Women's Participation in the Moravian Church in South-West Africa', in Oduyoye and Kanyoro 1990: 145-48.
Tappa, Louise
    1988   'The Christ-Event from the Viewpoint of African Women: A Protestant Perspective', in Fabella and Oduyoye 1988: 30-34.
Tetteh, Rachel
    1990a   'Woman', in Oduyoye and Kanyoro 1990: 227-29.
    1990b   'Women in the Church', in Oduyoye and Kanyoro 1990: 155-64.
    1997   'Regulating Women's Sexuality', in Amoah 1997: 51-62.
Tsabedze, Joyce
    1990   'Women in the Church', in Oduyoye and Kanyoro 1990: 76-79.
Umeagudosu, Margaret
    1997   'The Earth Belongs to God: Biblical Expositions through the Eyes of a Nigerian Woman', in Amoah 1997: 10-19.
Williams, Dolores
    1993   *Sisters in the Wilderness* (Maryknoll, NY: Orbis Books).

Index of Authors

FEMINIST THEOLOGY TITLES

i Other Books in the Introductions
in Feminist Theology Series

INTRODUCING ASIAN FEMINIST THEOLOGY
KWOK PUI-LAN

The book introduces the history, critical issues, and direction of feminist theology as a grass roots movement in Asia. Kwok Pui-Lan takes care to highlight the diversity of this broad movement, noting that not all women theologians in Asia embrace feminism. Amid a diverse range of sociopolitical, religiocultural, postcultural, and postcolonial context, this book lifts up the diversity of voices and ways of doing feminist theology while attending to women's experiences, how the Bible is interpreted, and the ways that Asian religious traditions are appropriated. It searches out a passionate, life-affirming spirituality through feminine images of God, new metaphors for Christ, and reformulation of sin and redemption.

ISBN 0 8298 1399-3   Paper/136 pages/$16.95

INTRODUCING THEALOGY: DISCOURSE ON THE GODDESS
MELISSA RAPHAEL

Introducing Thealogy provides an accessible but critical introduction to the relationship of religion, theo/alogy, and gender especially as these concepts unfold in the revival of Goddess religion among feminists in Europe, North America, and Australasia. Raphael focuses on the boundaries of that broad movement, what is meant by the Goddess, theology in history and ethics, the political implications of the movement, and how it relates to feminist witchcraft.

ISBN 0 8298 1379-9   Paper/184 pages/$17.95

INTRODUCING BODY THEOLOGY
LISA ISHERWOOD AND ELIZABETH STUART

Because Christianity asserts that God was incarnated in human form, one might expect that its theologies would be body affirming. Yet for women (and indeed also for gay men) the body has been the site for oppression. *Introducing Body Theology* offers a body-centered theology that discusses cosmology, ecology, ethics, immortality, and sexuality, in a concise introduction that proposes and encourages a positive theology of the body.

ISBN 0 8298 1375-6   Paper/168 pages/$16.95

INTRODUCING A PRACTICAL FEMINIST THEOLOGY OF WORSHIP
JANET WOOTTON

Only three great women-songs are retained in the Bible: Deborah's song for ordinary people, Hannah's song of triumph, and Mary's song at meeting her cousin Elizabeth.

Many others, such as Miriam's song, are truncated or overshadowed by male triumphs. *Introducing a Practical Feminist Theology of Worship* begins by revealing how women have been 'whispering liturgy'. It then explores female images of God, discusses how worship spaces function, and offers practical suggestions for how women can use words and movements to construct authentic forms of worship.

ISBN 0 8298 1405-1   Paper/148 pages/$16.95

INTRODUCING REDEMPTION IN CHRISTIAN FEMINISM
ROSEMARY R. RUETHER

Introducing Redemption in Christian Feminism explores the dichotomy between two patterns of thinking found in Christianity: the redemption of Christ being applied to all without regard to gender, and the exclusion of women from leadership because women were created subordinate to men and because women were more culpable for sin. After examining these two patterns, Ruether examines some key theological themes: Christology, the self, the cross, and eschatology.

ISBN 0 8298 1382-9   Paper/136 pages/$15.95

INTRODUCING FEMINIST IMAGES OF GOD
MARY GREY

Mary Grey presents recent thinking reflecting early attempts to move beyond restrictive God language, opening up the possibilities of more inclusive ways of praying. The rich experiences of God, distinctive and diverse, are seen through the eyes of many different cultures and the women who struggle for justice. Using the figure of Sophia Wisdom as an example, Grey shows that there are many still unplumbed images of God to discover.

ISBN 0 8298 1418-3   Paper/148 pages/$17.00

To order call 1-800-537-3394, fax 216-736-2206,
or visit our Web site at www.pilgrimpress.com.
(Prices do not include shipping and handling.) Prices subject to change without notice.